Controlling Anger

A solution focused approach for children

www.teachingexpertise.com/teachtoinspire

Acknowledgements:

The authors would like to thank the children and staff of Rabbsfarm Primary School for their support and co-operation in developing and delivering this programme.

Our memorable group deserve special thanks:

Billy

Curtis

Jack

Jordan

Trimaine.

Controlling Anger

A solution focused approach for children

Sara Daly and Tina Rae

This book is created by Barbara Maines and George Robinson for Teach To Inspire, a series for Optimus Education.

Authors

Sara Daly and Tina Rae

Designer

Jess Wright

Editors

Barbara Maines and George Robinson

Copy editor

Mel Maines

Illustrator

Tina Rae

Printed by Hobbs the Printers Ltd.

Registered Office: Brunel Road, Totton, Hampshire SO40 3WX, UK

Registered Number: 422 132

Published by Optimus Education: a division of Optimus Professional Publishing Limited

Registered office: 33-41 Dallington Street, London EC1V 0BB

Registered number: 05791519

Telephone: 0845 450 6407 Fax: 0845 450 6410

www.teachingexpertise.com

ISBN 978-1-906517-01-4

A CD-ROM is attached to the inside front cover and is an integral part of this publication.

Contents

Use of the CD-ROM

Many Teach to Inspire publications include CD-ROMs to support the purchaser in the delivery of the training or teaching activities. These may include any of the following file formats:

- PDFs requiring Acrobat v.3
- Microsoft Word files
- Microsoft PowerPoint files
- Video clips which can be played by Windows Media Player
- If games are included the software required is provided on the CD.

All material on the accompanying CD-ROM can be printed by the purchaser/user of the book. This includes library copies. Some of this material is also printed in the book and can be photocopied but this will restrict it to the black and white/greyscale version when there might be a colour edition on the CD-ROM.

The CD-ROM itself must not be reproduced or copied in its entirety for use by others without permission from the publisher.

All material on the CD-ROM is © Daly and Rae 2008.

Symbols key

 This symbol indicates a page that can be copied from the book or printed from the CD-ROM.

My Anger

At lunch the footballer savagely pushed me to the ground like a bowling pin.

The monster in my head began to wake up.

Quickly he grew stronger.

I could not control him any longer.

He ripped his cage open and found the control panel to my brain.

Getting in control, he pressed the destruct button.

He makes me shoot off like a missile seeking a target.

By Jack Culhane

Being Me

I fight and I steal,

Trimaine's my name,

Causing trouble is my game,

If I spit flame I'll turn you lame,

So I'll always be standing,

I'll never go down,

That is why I'm wearing this crown.

But now I realise,

That it is not wise to tell lies,

And fighting and stealing,

Won't get me anywhere with my dealings,

So now you see,

It is wrong to act like me!

By Trimaine Bailey

Note: The above poems, produced by students who participated in this programme, appear within the programme as copiable resources.

Controlling Anger

Introduction and Background

Introduction and Background

This programme is designed to be used in the primary phase and is aimed at students who experience difficulties in managing their behaviour within a range of school contexts. It aims to empower students to manage their behaviour and strong feelings more positively and to enable them to avoid situations of conflict. It promotes the belief that students can effect change and that it is possible to resolve difficulties and achieve a positive outcome.

The government's recent agenda for inclusion in schools and the focus on preventing and reducing exclusions has further raised awareness as to the specific need of some students with social, emotional and behavioural difficulties. This has led to teachers and support staff rethinking how such students are both supported and managed within the mainstream context. Under the Excellence and City initiatives, schools have been able to further access student referral units and learning support units alongside setting up on-site units and introducing and implementing Pastoral Support Plans (PSPs).

During recent years a plethora of programmes have been developed which aim to provide students with opportunities to develop their social, emotional and behavioural skills. As part of the Primary and Secondary National Strategies the DfES have also introduced the SEAL curriculum (Social and Emotional Aspects of Learning) in mainstream schools. The idea here is to develop pupils' ability to cope with difficult and uncomfortable situations and emotions, and also to focus upon further promoting pro-social and empathic behaviours within both the classroom and playground context. The success of the SEAL programme, alongside many other initiatives, is dependent upon whether or not the whole-school framework and policy for promoting positive behaviour and emotional literacy is in place and truly effective.

It does appear that approaches based on cognitive behavioural therapy and solution focused psychology generally appear to be effective in ensuring the inclusion of the most at risk students. However, there does seem to remain a group of harder to reach students who may well become permanently excluded from school and are subsequently required to attend a pupil referral unit prior to either being reintegrated into mainstream or accessing special provision. It is with this group of students in mind that the Controlling Anger programme has been developed. It was initially intended to support a group of 'at risk' pupils within the context of a mainstream primary school. Each of the pupils exhibited significant difficulties in managing their strong emotions and coping with conflict. All of the pupils appeared to have a history of aggressive and violent behaviour towards both peers and, at times, towards members of staff within the school context.

Staff in the school were keen to develop an emotionally literate approach and context in which to successfully engage with these pupils and also help to promote change to ensure that they remained within the mainstream context.

A preventative approach

This programme consequently aims to provide facilitators with a preventative approach to enable pupils to develop the skills that they need. It is primarily aimed at those pupils who are experiencing difficulty in managing their strong feelings and in managing conflict within both the school and home settings. It is, of course, envisaged that the school will have already worked on such difficulties with the pupils and that the school's Special Educational Needs (SEN) and pastoral systems will have worked closely together.

This work may have included parental involvement, systems for monitoring pupil progress, mentoring schemes, individual behaviour plans and some outside agency involvement. Typically, the pupils may have been identified, and usually placed, on Action Plus or School Action of the Code of Practice for Special Educational Needs.

The focus here is on helping the pupils to identify and recognise the triggers to anger, strong feelings and conflict and then to support them in developing positive strategies to manage such feelings and the types of problems that they might regularly be experiencing, particularly in the school context. The course is designed to be used with a group of between 6 and 10 pupils.

Mental health and the concept of emotional literacy

It is important to highlight the fact that many pupils for whom this programme was initially developed will have encountered difficult situations in the past and problems in a range of contexts. These negative experiences, alongside frequent rejections by adults and peers, may have led to aggressive or withdrawn behaviours. For some of the pupils targeted, there may also have been a degree of depression. In the light of these experiences, it could be appropriate to describe the pupils as not being particularly 'mentally healthy'.

A study by the Mental Health Foundation (The Big Picture, February 1999) focused upon the promotion of children and young people's mental health. The report defined the mentally healthy as those with the ability to:

- initiate, develop and sustain mutually satisfying personal relationships
- use and enjoy solitude
- develop psychologically, emotionally, creatively, intellectually and spiritually
- become aware of others and empathise with them
- develop a sense of right and wrong
- play and learn
- face problems and setbacks and learn from them in ways appropriate for the child's age.

The report also identified the fact that since the 1940s, the number of children experiencing mental ill health had increased to 1 in 5. Such a statistic may well have been one of the drivers behind the DfES Social, Emotional and Behavioral Skills (SEBS) curriculum which aims to address and develop the emotional, social and behavioural needs of young people in schools. Such resources also aim to promote an emotionally literate and mentally healthy school context and environment in which teachers and pupils can successfully learn and work together. This is certainly a laudable aim. However, for some individuals, as stated earlier, it will be advisable to provide something in addition to such an approach. This will be necessary in order to ensure that the students can develop the kinds of skills that they need in order to remain successfully within the mainstream context.

Different types of learning

Dealing with our emotions in terms of both relating to ourselves and to others is clearly a complex issue. Individuals tend to need both educational and skill-based learning in order to gain the skills that they need to be effective socially, emotionally and academically. Sunderland and Engleheart (1993) state that 'It is a mockery to say that a person's emotional life takes care of itself. It clearly does not.' (page 2). This programme therefore aims to provide this kind of skill-based learning. The sessions focus specifically on teaching young people the kinds of self-management and emotional control skills that they will need in order to be able to cope effectively in both the school and social contexts.

Psychologists have identified two types of learning: cognitive learning (which involves absorbing new data and gaining insights into existing frameworks of association) and emotional learning. It is the latter that appears to involve engaging the part of the brain where our emotional signature is stored. This demands much of the individual and specifically involves new ways of thinking. Cognitive learning appears to be more straightforward whereas emotional learning is clearly more complex and difficult. For example, it is harder for an individual to accept the fact that they may need to improve their anger management skills than it might be to engage them in learning a new cognitive skill such as a new computer programme.

Dann (2001) states that the prospect of needing to develop greater emotional intelligence is likely to generate some resistance to change. It isn't easy to accept the fact that you need to make such changes. This factor has been taken into account when formulating the Controlling Anger programme. The programme focuses throughout on promoting, fostering and motivating pupils to effect change. The sessions utilise solution focused processes and encourage the pupils to continually self-reflect, self-monitor and set realistic and achievable targets and goals. There is a continual focus upon reflecting on key skills and identifying ways of changing unhelpful patterns of behaviour. The solution focused approach is particularly powerful. It is described by Rhodes and Ajmal (1995) as being a significant and incredibly useful tool in supporting students through the process of change. They state that, 'In supporting students... in their wish to change what is happening, we have found no model of approaching behaviour difficulties more useful and flexible than solution focused thinking,' (page 55). This seems to be because this kind of process encourages pupils to formulate a new and more positive story for themselves. This is one way in which their skills, strengths and resources can be both identified and reinforced. They can move away from merely focusing upon the negatives and difficulties to a position where they can consider and visualise a more positive outcome for themselves, identifying the kinds of resources and strategies that they would need in order to be more effective. This process is utilised throughout the whole programme in order to support pupils in effecting positive change for themselves.

There is a companion programme for older children available. The opportunity to participate once in the primary phase and again in the secondary phase will certainly be of benefit to some students.

Objectives of the Course

The series of lessons has been designed to meet the following objectives:

- to encourage students to develop an awareness of their own feelings

- to enable and encourage students to become reflective regarding their own behaviour and the consequences of that behaviour

- to enable students to label feelings and know when they may or may not affect both work and relationships

- to enable students to further develop personal insight

- to develop students' self-esteem and self-confidence

- to enable students to accept and utilise constructive structured criticism and feedback

- to encourage students to develop their own self-control and self-management strategies

- to encourage students to develop empathy and authenticity

- to enable students to develop flexibility in order to cope more effectively with change and new systems and ways of doing things

- to help students develop internal locus of control, i.e. to encourage them to have a sense of control over their own actions

- to encourage students to develop self-motivation, resilience and a positive attitude

- to encourage students to learn and make use of alternatives to physical or verbal aggression and to express their feelings and views in a more positive and assertive way

- to encourage parents/carers and school staff to adopt a consistent approach in terms of developing students' emotional literacy, social skills and self-esteem

- to promote partnership working between home and school so as to ensure a consistent approach

- to further enable and encourage school staff to review current policy and practice in terms of managing the emotional, social and behavioural needs of students in their care

- to promote a positive ethos and climate in which the notion of change becomes a positive daily reality.

The extent to which these objectives are met may well be the best indicator as to the success or otherwise of this programme.

The Structure of the Programme

The programme is divided into 10 sessions as follows:

Session 1: Introduction

Setting of ground rules.

Introducing the assault cycle.

Focusing on current strategies.

Introducing the strong feelings diary.

Session 2: Fighting Friends

Questions for reflection on the emotional story describing how two friends fall out when one becomes jealous of the other's friendship with a new pupil.

Top tips for Josie.

Designing anger models with reference to Novaco's Firework Model.

Session 3: The Loss

Questions for reflection on the article describing a girl who has lost her Gran and believes none of her friends understands how she feels. When they try to talk to her she swears at them.

Identifying triggers, thoughts and feelings.

Utilising the traffic lights to solve problems.

Session 4: Cussing

Questions for reflection on the emotional story describing how a boy insults another pupils mother after she says his mother is a show off. The girl finally snaps and slaps the boy before running out of class.

Identifying early warning signs.

Strategies for letting off steam and creating new scripts.

Session 5: Feeling Stupid

Questions for reflection on the emotional story describing how a child is made to feel stupid in front of his class. The boy becomes so upset that he lashes out at the pupil who called him stupid.

Time-out strategy.

Using problem cards.

Introduction of the problem solving framework.

Session 6: The Foul

Questions for reflection on the emotional story describing how a girl is tackled badly on the football pitch and then decides to get her own back when the referee does nothing, ruining her chances of being chosen by the talent scout.

Using 'I' messages.

Talking through problems.

Using a problem-solving sheet.

Session 7: Bully Boys

Questions for reflection on the emotional story describing how a boy who is being bullied finally snaps one day and repeatedly kicks one of the bullies.

Self-reflection on personal triggers.

Using the bully box and identifying further strategies.

Session 8: Listen-up

Questions for reflection on the emotional story describing how a teacher refuses to listen to a group of pupils or help them in their work. This leads to a great feeling of frustration and results in the teacher's desk being kicked.

Checking up on our skills using the strong feelings log.

Introducing the tension scale.

Session 9: All Alone

Questions for reflection on the emotional story describing how a new pupil at a school feels so isolated that he becomes an elective mute. The anger and jealousy continue to build until he explodes and starts a fight with another boy.

Strategy information sheet on stress and anger management.

Identifying ways to dampen the fuse.

Introducing a new script and personal strategy sheet.

Introduction of a relaxation script.

Session 10: Review and Evaluation

Completion of the post-course observation checklist by staff.

Thoughtstorm activity and completion of course evaluation sheet.

Setting top targets.

Award ceremony.

The Structure of the Sessions

The sessions are usually structured in a similar way. The pre-course assessment should be completed before the start of the course. This can be done individually with the targeted pupils. We would suggest that the facilitator reads each statement to the pupil and elicits their responses verbally. This will allow for an explanation of any new concepts/language. This is extremely important, as it is a means by which the pupils can measure their own progress both before and after this intervention. The introductory session also follows a distinctive format in that the facilitator is required to formulate group rules for the course with the students alongside introducing the main aims and content of the course and the use of the strong feelings diary.

Apart from the first and final session the sessions tend to follow the same format as follows:

Introduction

The facilitator can write the main aims onto a white board or flip chart, or simply read through these from the session plan provided as appropriate.

Circle warm-up

Circle warm-up activities are generally intended to set a positive and relaxed ethos for the sessions. They usually make use of the Circle Time approach and encourage pupils to develop both social and emotional skills within a safe and secure context.

Strong feelings diary review

At the start of each session the pupils have the opportunity to review their progress during the previous week. They are asked to discuss how they coped with any difficult situations and to record any outbursts of anger in terms of triggers, feelings, behaviours and consequences. They are also asked to scale themselves on how well they coped with the escalation of anger on a scale of 0 – 10. This sharing process aims to develop empathy and encourages the pupils to share their strategies and means of coping most effectively.

Emotional story

The facilitator then reads the emotional story to the group. Each of these articles details how a child loses control and behaves in an inappropriate way, i.e. they do not get the best possible outcome for themselves. This is a safe way for the pupils to explore their strong feelings of anger/loss/jealousy as they are asked to identify with a fictional character rather than initially self-reflect upon their own behaviours. The fact that the characters who tend to lose control of their feelings are children is also significant. The idea here is to reinforce the fact that children can have difficulties with their strong feelings. The articles are intended to raise awareness as to the negative outcomes of such behaviours and the importance for all of us of developing the emotional control and strategies that we need in order to be able to cope most effectively in a range of contexts.

Question sheet

The pupils are then encouraged to analyse the character behaviours and the possible feelings and emotions that they may have triggered by their outbursts of angry and out of control behaviour. This is done by focusing upon a series of questions. The essential aim here is to encourage the pupils to suggest what strategies could have been used by the characters involved in order to de-escalate their feelings of anger.

Strategy and problem-solving sheets

The pupils are then encouraged to complete a series of reflection and problem solving activity sheets. These are different in each session but generally utilise solution focused approaches and principles and encourage the pupils to develop their personal skills and strategies. These can then be used in the coming week to help the pupils to modify their own behaviours and become more self-reflective and in control.

We have also produced a letter for parents/carers to describe in brief the overall aims and objectives of the course and the contents of each session. This letter and summary can be provided at the outset and parents/carers should be encouraged to support their pupils in keeping the strong feelings diary on a weekly basis. It is also be important to encourage them to discuss, in a non-judgemental and non-accusatory manner, how well things are going with the child, identifying and highlighting the most positive strategies that they have been using during the week.

Using the programme – a note for facilitators

Although this programme has been developed within the context of a mainstream primary school and subsequently used with small groups, it would be feasible to adapt the resources as appropriate for larger groups of pupils, i.e. the programme could form the basis of the whole-class project or a supplement to the many areas of the SEAL curriculum. However, it should be highlighted that the main focus of this programme is on supporting pupils between the ages of 8 and 12 years to develop their ability to manage strong feelings more effectively. It may therefore be most appropriate to make use of this resource as originally intended. We would suggest that groups of 8 to 10 pupils supported by two adults seem to benefit best from this type of approach. This allows for a smaller, more nurturing and less judgemental climate to be set. The central aim here is to attempt to engage each of the pupils by recognising and validating their experiences and encouraging them to subsequently empathise with others who are experiencing similar difficulties.

When trialling this programme for the first time it was possible to allocate the Special Educational Needs Co-ordinator (SENCO) and the Educational Psychologist to the target group in order to deliver each of the sessions. These individuals were then able to provide ongoing 1:1 mentoring support for individual pupils and liaise regularly with their parents alongside delivering the programme. However, we recognise that it doesn't necessarily follow that the same arrangement should or could be made in other contexts.

Once this programme has been completed, it is anticipated that the majority of the pupils will have developed some of the skills that they need in order to cope more effectively in the mainstream context. However, it will be helpful to provide ongoing support and to ensure that systems for monitoring and supporting individual pupils are clarified at the outset.

This may well need to involve additional input from the SEN team or from pastoral staff within the school. It is hoped that this programme will build upon current good practice in mainstream classrooms, specifically the work covered within the SEAL curriculum. Its basis in solution focused processes, interactions and emotional wellbeing initiatives will hopefully provide teachers with a dynamic and successful way forward in terms of ensuring the inclusion of some of our more vulnerable and sometimes 'out of control' children.

It is further hoped that the course will have impacted positively on increasing staff awareness of the nature of strong feelings and how these can be managed most effectively. Running away from them and hiding from them is simply not feasible. We need to demystify these more uncomfortable feelings and address them in a positive and solution focused way. School staff may consider the need to increase staff awareness of self-management issues and approaches in order to then further develop a whole-school policy and approach. Staff may identify implications for whole-school staff training, perhaps in the area of counselling skills and related issues, the appointment of mentoring and counselling staff and the development of a peer counselling process alongside further review of the PSHE curriculum. This may involve developing opportunities for listening environments and appropriate resources and materials to ensure the mental and emotional wellbeing of all in the school context.

Links to the SEAL curriculum

The eight stories in this programme are not only intended to develop the pupils emotional literacy but specifically their ability to manage and control strong feelings. They are also intended to reinforce some of the key themes and concepts introduced via the Primary National Strategy's SEAL curriculum. Within the stories and the associated solution focused activities there are clear links to the 'new beginnings' theme. For example, the pupils are frequently asked to imagine how they could react better or differently in the future in a similar situation. They are asked to visualise life without the problem and to understand the fact that change is always possible, i.e. they can always make a new start, a fresh beginning, a new resolution, etc.

The stories are also linked to the theme of friendship and the way in which friends can both support and reject each other. They particularly focus upon the need to be self-reflective about one's behaviour while also empathising with others, i.e. developing the ability to correctly judge and gauge how others are feeling and how they are responding or reacting to your own behaviour. There is a clear link to the themes of resolving conflict and making good choices. This is particularly apparent in the ways in which the pupils are encouraged to identify what would be the best option in each of the scenarios presented, i.e. how could the character have achieved a better outcome, behaved differently and managed their strong feelings of anger, stress or aggression more effectively?

The notion of taking responsibility is also a key theme running throughout the stories alongside developing the ability to problem solve. The pupils are frequently made aware of the fact that being able to solve problems is a key social skill and one that they need to develop in order to be effective in the social context. There are some links to the theme of coping with change, for example the new girl starting school; someone having to cope with a new teacher or someone losing their Gran. The idea here is to once again build on this particular SEAL theme, encouraging the pupils to think about how they can cope with loss more effectively and how they can plan ahead in order to cope with changes that they will experience on a daily basis.

Most important is the link to the key theme of self-awareness. The pupils are encouraged throughout these sessions to increase their own levels of self-awareness, to reflect upon their own behaviours and to remain solution focused, i.e. adopting the mantra that it is good to be me and I can always change and improve my behaviour.

References

Breakwell, GM. (1997) *Coping with Aggressive Behaviour*, Leicester: British Psychological Society.

Boulger, E. (2002) *Building on Social Skills*, Staffordshire, NASEN.

Casey, J. (2002) *Getting it Right: A Behaviour Curriculum*, London, A Lucky Duck Book, Sage.

Dann, J. (2001) *Emotional Intelligence in a Week*, Oxford, Hodder and Stoughton.

De Shazar, S. (1988) *Clues: Investigating Solutions in Brief Therapy*, New York, Norton.

Elias, M. J. and Clabby, J. (1992) *Building Social and Emotional Development in Deaf Children*, The PATH Programme, Seattle, University of California Press.

Faupel, A., Herrick E. & Sharp, P. (1998) *Solution Talk: Hosting Therapeutic Conversations*, New York, Norton.

Goleman, E. (1995) *Emotional Intelligence: Why it can matter more than IQ*. London, Bloomsbury.

Gourley, P. (1999) *Teaching Self-control in the Classroom: a Cognitive Behavioural Approach*, London, A Lucky Duck Book, Sage.

Greenberg, M. T. and Kushche, C. A. (1993) *Promoting Social and Emotional Development in Deaf Children*, The PATH Programme, Seattle, University of California Press.

Johnson, P. & Rae, T. (1999) *Crucial Skills: An Anger Management and Problem Solving Teaching Programme for High School Students*, London, A Lucky Duck Book, Sage.

Marris, B. & Rae, T. (2006) *Teaching Anger Management and Problem Solving Skills*, London, A Lucky Duck Book, Sage.

Rae, T. (1998) *Dealing with Feeling*, London, A Lucky Duck Book, Sage.

Rae, T. (2000) *Confidence, Assertiveness, Self-Esteem: A Series of Twelve Sessions for Secondary School Students*, London, A Lucky Duck Book, Sage.

Rae, T. (2001) *Strictly Stress: Effective Stress Management for High School Students*, London, A Lucky Duck Book, Sage.

Rae, T. & Marris, B. (2004) *Escape from Exclusion*, London, A Lucky Duck Book, Sage.

Rhodes, J. & Ajimal, Y. (1995) *Solution focused Thinking in Schools*, London, Brief Therapy Publication.

Sheldon, B. (1995) *Cognitive Behavioural Therapy: Research, Practice and Philosophy*, London, Routledge.

Sunderland, M. & Engleheart, P. (1993) *Draw on your Emotions*, Oxford, Speechmark.

Warden, E. & Christie, E. (1997) *Teaching Social Behaviour*, London, David Fulton Publishers.

Wardle, C. and Rae, T. (2002) *School Survival – Helping Students Survive and Succeed in Secondary School*, London, A Lucky Duck Book, Sage.

White, M. (1999) *Picture This: Guided Imagery for Circle Time*, London, A Lucky Duck Book, Sage.

Getting Started

Pupil selection

This course has been trialled with small groups of between 6 and 8 pupils. Pupils have generally been selected by the class teacher in consultation with the school's SENCO and Educational Psychologist. In the group work conducted to date we have found it useful to ensure a balance of pupils within the group, i.e. some who are displaying some difficulties in managing their own behaviours and emotions and others who can act as good role models, having developed age-appropriate social and emotional skills. In order to select pupils for the course it is useful to make use of the observation checklist. Staff can rate individual pupils against 20 specific categories. For example, he or she comes to school or class happily, they settle in class without distracting or hurting other children and control their anger when provoked, etc. It is possible for a pupil to be awarded a worst score of 80 and a best score of 20 on this checklist. The 20 categories are key areas for focusing upon within the course. We have found it useful for both pupils and the facilitator to complete the observation checklist.

Pre-course assessment

Once the pupils have been selected it is also helpful for each individual to complete a pre-course assessment. This assessment covers four key areas as follows: 'What I Know About My Anger', 'Skills I Currently Have', 'What I Hope to Learn' and 'Changes I Need to Make'. The pupils are asked to rate themselves against a series of statements on a scale of $0 - 10$, 0 equalling not very much or never, 5 equalling a medium amount or sometimes and 10 equalling a lot or almost always. They are asked to consider their current level of knowledge as to what makes them angry, what makes others angry and how they cope in a range of difficult and highly emotional situations. This also provides them with an opportunity to begin to self-reflect and set realistic targets and goals for themselves. It is helpful for them to revisit this pre-course assessment once they have completed the course. Pupils can compare their ratings in terms of identifying skills development over this period of time. The course evaluation also provides them with an opportunity to rate each aspect of the course and to provide the course facilitators with ideas as to how the course could be improved if delivered again in the future.

The pre-course assessment is an essential element of the programme. It is vital for the pupils to begin to develop skills of self-reflection and to also identify reasonable and realistic goals for themselves. We would therefore strongly recommend that the facilitator conducts both the pre-course assessment and the course evaluation with each pupil on an individual basis. Although this may seem time consuming, we have found it to be the most effective means of eliciting the pupils' views and ensuring their understanding of key concepts.

Preparing parents/carers

It is essential that parents/carers agree that their children participate in the programme. It is also important that they are included from the outset in terms of being kept informed about the contents of the programme and included in the activities on an ongoing basis.

An example of a letter informing parents/carers of the nature and contents of the course is provided. Staff may wish to adapt this to suit their own purposes. Alternatively, the letter can be photocopied and sent out in the existing format. The letter describes the main contents of the course and specifically focuses upon the completion of the weekly feelings diary. This is important given the fact that parents/carers will be asked to support their children in recording these situations and beginning to reflect upon their responses and reactions. Parents/carers can also be provided with a summary of each of the 10 sessions. This highlights the skills being focused upon within the session while indentifying specific strategies that the children are being asked to make use of.

Equipment

Students who join the programme should bring (or be supplied with) a ring-binder for filing course work.

Controlling Anger

Pre-course Assessment

Resources to photocopy or print from the CD-ROM

Pre-course Assessment

Observation Checklist (Staff)

Letter to Parents/Carers

Course Programme

My Anger Poem.

Controlling Anger

Pre-course Assessment

What skills do I have?

What do I hope to learn?

What changes do I need to make?

Name:..

Date completed:...

Observation Checklist

Name..

Date of birth...

School...

Please circle the number which your observations suggest is most appropriate and add any comments that you think are important.

	Always	Usually	Some-times	Never	Comment
1. Comes to school/class happily	1	2	3	4	
2. Settles in class without fuss	1	2	3	4	
3. Settles in small groups easily	1	2	3	4	
4. Follows class routines	1	2	3	4	
5. Accepts teacher's directions	1	2	3	4	
6. Accepts other pupils taking the lead	1	2	3	4	
7. Appears popular with other children	1	2	3	4	
8. Has at least one good friend	1	2	3	4	
9. Plays appropriately with other children	1	2	3	4	
10. Copes well with disappointment	1	2	3	4	
11. Appears confident	1	2	3	4	
12. Feels good about themselves	1	2	3	4	
13. Concentrates well	1	2	3	4	
14. Controls anger when provoked	1	2	3	4	
15. Has insight into own behaviour	1	2	3	4	
16. Learns from mistakes	1	2	3	4	
17. Keeps hands, feet, objects to themselves	1	2	3	4	
18. Hurts self	4	3	2	1	
19. Distracts other children	4	3	2	1	
20. Hurts other children	4	3	2	1	
Total					

Best score = 20   Worst score = 80

Completed by ....

Date ....

Pre-course

Controlling Anger
Pre-course assessment

Rate yourself against each of the following statements on a scale of 0 – 10
(0 = not very much/never: 5 = a medium amount/sometimes: 10 = a lot/almost always).

My knowledge – what do I know about my anger?

I understand why I get angry.

| 0 | 1 | 2 | 3 | 4 | 5 | 6 | 7 | 8 | 9 | 10 |

Not very much   almost always

I understand why others get angry.

| 0 | 1 | 2 | 3 | 4 | 5 | 6 | 7 | 8 | 9 | 10 |

I know the triggers that start my anger.

| 0 | 1 | 2 | 3 | 4 | 5 | 6 | 7 | 8 | 9 | 10 |

I know how to stop my anger escalating.

| 0 | 1 | 2 | 3 | 4 | 5 | 6 | 7 | 8 | 9 | 10 |

I know what happens to my body when I get angry.

| 0 | 1 | 2 | 3 | 4 | 5 | 6 | 7 | 8 | 9 | 10 |

I understand the pattern of my angry outbursts.

| 0 | 1 | 2 | 3 | 4 | 5 | 6 | 7 | 8 | 9 | 10 |

I know that I can cope when other students get angry.

| 0 | 1 | 2 | 3 | 4 | 5 | 6 | 7 | 8 | 9 | 10 |

I know that I can cope when adults get angry

| 0 | 1 | 2 | 3 | 4 | 5 | 6 | 7 | 8 | 9 | 10 |

Pre-course

My skills – how are my skills now?

I can think about my behaviours and why I did what I did.

```
0        1        2        3        4        5        6        7        8        9        10
└────────┴────────┴────────┴────────┴────────┴────────┴────────┴────────┴────────┴────────┘
```

I can set sensible targets for change.

```
0        1        2        3        4        5        6        7        8        9        10
└────────┴────────┴────────┴────────┴────────┴────────┴────────┴────────┴────────┴────────┘
```

I can plan ahead.

```
0        1        2        3        4        5        6        7        8        9        10
└────────┴────────┴────────┴────────┴────────┴────────┴────────┴────────┴────────┴────────┘
```

I have a system to solve my problems.

```
0        1        2        3        4        5        6        7        8        9        10
└────────┴────────┴────────┴────────┴────────┴────────┴────────┴────────┴────────┴────────┘
```

I can use self-calming strategies (e.g. counting, deep breathing, relaxation).

```
0        1        2        3        4        5        6        7        8        9        10
└────────┴────────┴────────┴────────┴────────┴────────┴────────┴────────┴────────┴────────┘
```

I can talk myself down.

```
0        1        2        3        4        5        6        7        8        9        10
└────────┴────────┴────────┴────────┴────────┴────────┴────────┴────────┴────────┴────────┘
```

I can use time out properly.

```
0        1        2        3        4        5        6        7        8        9        10
└────────┴────────┴────────┴────────┴────────┴────────┴────────┴────────┴────────┴────────┘
```

I can use 'I' messages.

```
0        1        2        3        4        5        6        7        8        9        10
└────────┴────────┴────────┴────────┴────────┴────────┴────────┴────────┴────────┴────────┘
```

I can problem solve with friends.

```
0        1        2        3        4        5        6        7        8        9        10
└────────┴────────┴────────┴────────┴────────┴────────┴────────┴────────┴────────┴────────┘
```

Pre-course

I can problem solve with adults.

0   1   2   3   4   5   6   7   8   9   10

I can manage my stress.

0   1   2   3   4   5   6   7   8   9   10

I can understand how others are feeling and change my behaviours towards them if I think they are getting angry.

0   1   2   3   4   5   6   7   8   9   10

What do you hope to learn on this course?

* ....

* ....

* ....

* ....

How do you feel about your ability to manage your feelings and behaviour?
(0 = negative: 5 = OK: 10 = positive)

0   1   2   3   4   5   6   7   8   9   10

negative   positive

How would you like to feel about your ability to manage your feelings and behaviour in the future?

0   1   2   3   4   5   6   7   8   9   10

What do you think needs to change in order for you to make more progress? (Include things about yourself, others and your situation.)

Pre-Course

Letter to Parents/Carers

Dear Parents/Carers,

Your child has been selected to participate in a self-management programme called Controlling Anger. The main purpose of this course is to teach your child a variety of skills and strategies to enable them to express and control their more difficult feelings (including anger) in a more positive way.

There are a total of ten sessions in the course. During each session the pupils will examine a story that details how a person faces the consequences of an uncontrolled outburst of physical or verbal violence. Pupils are then encouraged to analyse the behaviour of the people in the story, looking at how the circumstances could have resulted in a very different outcome for the people involved if they had maintained a calmer attitude. Pupils are then introduced to calming strategies and skills and encouraged to decide how they could practically apply them to their own lives.

Possibly the most important aspect of the course is the completion of a weekly strong feelings diary. Pupils are asked to record any situations in terms of:

- The trigger – what made them feel angry, upset or stressed?
- Feelings – how did they feel at the time?
- Behaviour – what did they do in reaction to their feelings?
- Consequences – what happened as a result of their behaviour?
- Rating – pupils rate the outburst on a scale of 0 (really bad) to 10 (really good)

It would be extremely helpful if you could make the time to discuss your child's day with them and help them to complete their diary every evening. If your child has managed to use any of the skills or strategies to prevent an outburst, it would be brilliant if you could give them praise – a 'Fantastic, well done' or 'I am really proud of you' does wonders for reinforcing the use of the learnt skills and strategies.

So that you have a good idea of the strategies and skills we will be encouraging your child to use, we have provided you with a weekly breakdown of the course. If your child does have an outburst of anger or experiences a high level of stress, it may help if you discuss what strategies or skills they could have used to calm themselves before reaching the point at which they may have lost control.

We hope this explains how we are trying to help your child with their self-management and how you as parents/carers can support both them and us.

Yours sincerely

Pre-course

Course Programme

Session	Skills	Strategies
1. Introduction	Identify the body's physical reactions to anger and stress.	How 'dampening their fuse' by identifying calming strategies pupils currently use.
2. Fighting Friends	Identify own anger 'triggers' (what situations make pupils angry).	How to avoid 'trigger' situation and de-escalate feelings of anger..
3. The Loss	Analyse a trigger situation from a different perspective.	View 'trigger' situations as a fuse to anger. Introduce the traffic lights system of: stop and think, wait and plan and go.
4. Cursing	Identify the body's early warning signs that demonstrate growing feelings of anger, tension or stress.	Letting off steam – counting to ten and blowing out the anger.
5. Feeling Stupid	Reinforce analysing a trigger situation from a different perspective.	Time out – to discuss and reflect on feelings/trigger situations /examine situation from another perspective.
6. The Foul	Identify self-management strategies and methods that impact positively on behaviour.	Writing 'I' messages that support pupils to analyse a 'trigger' situation and suggest possible solutions.
7. Bully Boys	Use reflective skills to analyse 'trigger' situations therefore allowing them to remove themselves from a situation before their anger gets out of control.	Use physical exercise to 'let off steam'.
8. Listen-up!	Analyse how their behaviour may be a 'trigger' for other people's anger.	Use the tension scale as a stepped approach to calming down. The scale allows pupils to implement small stepped strategies to de-escalate their anger – move from 10 to 0
9. All Alone	Examine the effects that stress has on our behaviour.	Helping pupils to develop a personal script to enable them to stop, wait, reflect and go during high stress situations.
10. Review and Evaluation	Pupils analyse the effects and usefulness of the strategies and skills they have learnt over the course of the programme. This session also provides pupils with an opportunity to plan ahead and establish behaviour management targets for themselves.	

Pre-course

My Anger

At lunch the footballer savagely pushed me to the
ground like a bowling pin.

The monster in my head began to wake up.

Quickly he grew stronger.

I could not control him any longer.

He ripped his cage open and found the control
panel to my brain.

Getting in control, he pressed the destruct button.

He makes me shoot off like a missile seeking
a target.

By Jack Culhane

Controlling Anger

Session 1
Introduction

Resources to photocopy or print from the CD-ROM

Group Rules

Circle Time Tags

How Do I Feel?

The Assault Cycle

Keeping Calm

My Strong Feelings Diary: Week 1

Session 1: Introduction

Group session – 45 minutes to 1 hour

Setting the scene

In order for the programme to run smoothly it is essential to establish a set of group rules and to briefly examine the main objectives of the course. It will be important to create a positive atmosphere and to ensure that all pupils involved in this course understand the primary objective of the sessions: to provide them with useful and practical strategies to effect positive changes and manage themselves more effectively within a range of potentially volatile contexts.

The facilitator can briefly outline the main aims and purpose of the course. This includes helping pupils to:

- identify and understand anger triggers and triggers to other strong emotions
- understand consequences of expressing strong feelings in an inappropriate manner
- become more aware of physical reactions to expressing strong feelings
- identify methods they may use to calm themselves after becoming angry, upset or stressed
- identify how they feel once they have managed to calm down
- identify methods they may use or be aware of to prevent uncontrolled loss of temper.

Activity One – Group rules

To enable pupils to claim ownership of the group rules it is extremely important that they are given enough time to discuss and agree their own set of rules. By ensuring that pupils have ownership of their rules it will help considerably towards establishing a workable code of conduct that they will adhere to in each of the sessions.

The group rules may include ideas from the following:

- An undertaking to keep all discussions within the group private – this will build upon the Circle Time rules that are operating within many schools.
- To all try and contribute equally within every group session.
- An agreement to not criticise or put each other down.
- To try and respect each other's point of view.
- An undertaking to try to work together co-operatively.
- An undertaking to be kind and supportive towards each other.
- A promise that all within the group will try to maintain a positive solution-focused attitude and problem solve rather than be negative.

Once the group have decided upon the rules that they feel are essential to the smooth running of the sessions, the facilitator can record them on the appropriate activity sheet provided in this session plan. Alternatively, pupils could design and illustrate their own worksheets or work co-operatively as a group to create a poster that illustrates the agreed rules.

It is essential that these rules are reinforced throughout this session. Allow a little time at the beginning of each subsequent session to revisit the group rules and reinforce the importance of abiding by them.

Activity Two – Circle time tags

This can be organised if the facilitator acts, as a scribe for the pupils ideas/thoughts. Pupils may like to conduct this aspect of the session verbally within a Circle Time session. This method requires a much more 'hands on' approach from the facilitator, who introduces the question and then models the answer for the pupils. The facilitator can provide pupils with opening sentences that they are required to finish:

- When I get mad, it's usually because...
- When I get mad, I want to...
- When I get mad, my body feels...
- When I get mad, it helps me to calm down if I...
- When I get mad, it helps to talk to...
- After I've been mad, I feel...
- To prevent getting mad, I could...

Activity Three – How do I feel?

The next activity in this session encourages pupils to recognise and examine the physical signs/reactions they experience as their anger escalates.

Seated in a circle, pupils can discuss the activity sheet provided and identify their own physical indicators and reactions to escalating anger:

- I feel hot.
- My hands start to sweat.
- I find it difficult to stay still, I get all fidgety.
- My mouth gets dry.
- My hands go into fists.
- My body feels tense.
- My heart races.
- I breathe more quickly.
- I feel panicky.

The facilitator may have to prompt pupils to identify additional physical indicators that they experience as their anger escalates. Although an activity sheet has been provided the majority of this activity could be conducted verbally if pupils have significant difficulties with the recording process.

Activity Four – The assault cycle

To help pupils to understand their anger effectively, it is essential that they recognise how anger is a cycle of assault.

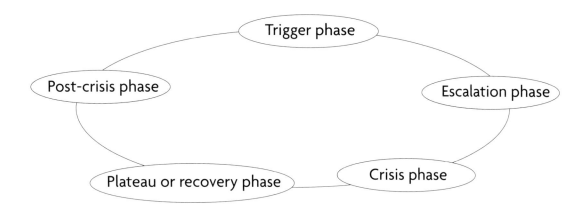

Pupils examine the handout illustrating Breakwell's (1997) graph depicting the assault cycle. It is important to discuss the actual phases that an outburst of anger passes through and how this affects the individual;

- Trigger phase – the event that ignites a person's fuse.
- Escalation phase – where the body is preparing for fight or flight.
- Crisis phase – when the person can not make any rational judgements or show any empathy for others. This leads to the outburst.
- Plateau or recovery phase – this is the vulnerable stage when it is easy to re-escalate the problem.
- Post-crisis phase – at this point pupils could become depressed as a result of their outburst.

The use of the graph provides pupils with a very visual representation of how their feeling of anger progresses.

Activity Five – Keeping calm

Having examined the assault cycle and the physical and emotional effects that it can and does have upon them, it is important for pupils to investigate how they can practically 'dampen their fuses'. This activity can be conducted by the facilitator, working through the accompanying activity sheet with the group within a Circle Time set-up. The facilitator can prompt and model appropriate responses by providing opening sentences for the pupils to complete.

Alternatively, pupils can work through the accompanying worksheet independently and then all answers could be drawn together during a Circle Time feedback session. Using this method will of course be dependent upon the pupils' academic ability or willingness to put pen to paper. If this is not appropriate to the group or writing would cause the pupils to become unfocused or alienated do not pursue or insist on written answers. This would just make pupils unwilling to contribute further in this session and perhaps in future sessions.

In this activity, pupils review a list of calming strategies that people use in order to help them to calm down when they recognise the feelings that accompany anger:

1. Walking away from the incident.

2. Counting to ten.

3. Talking yourself into feeling calm.

4. Using a catchphrase.

5. Pretending to be somewhere else.

6. Hiding behind an imaginary shield.

7. Using the turtle technique and protecting yourself inside your shell.

8. Taking some exercise – running, football, shooting baskets.

9. Having a special place to go.

10. Having a special person to be with.

11. Listening to music.

12. Breathing deeply and slowly.

13. Relaxing clenched muscles.

The facilitator may have to prompt pupils to identify the three strategies that may be most useful to them.

It may be useful at this point to discuss the advantages and disadvantages of each calming strategy. Once pupils have identified the three strategies that they may find helpful in controlling their anger outbursts, they should be encouraged to explore what other strategies may help them to prevent an outburst of anger in the future.

Activity Six – My strong feelings diary

Pupils are introduced to the feelings diary. A format is provided, which they will be asked to complete during the coming week. They will be required to record any outburst of anger in terms of:

• Triggers – what made them angry, upset or stressed?

• Feelings – when they became angry, upset or stressed what feelings/reactions did they notice within themselves?

• Behaviour – what they did when they experienced an escalation of strong feelings.

• Consequences – what happened next?

They are also asked to scale themselves on how well they coped with the escalation in strong feelings as marks out of 10.

0	5	10
Not well	OK	Brilliant

Plenary

The facilitator can prompt the pupils to review the session. It may be useful to focus on the following questions:

- What did you learn in this session?
- How do you feel about this session?
- How do you think this session might help you in the future?
- What advice would you give us if we ran this session again?

At the close of the session pupils are given a copy of the strong feelings diary in the format provided. This diary can then be reviewed in the next session within a Circle Time discussion.

Group Rules for the Controlling Anger Course

These are our rules and we all agree to try and keep them:

-
-
-
-
-

Signed ....

Circle Time Tags

• When I get mad, it's usually because..

• When I get mad, I want to...

• When I get mad, my body feels..

• When I get mad, it helps me to calm down if I...

• When I get mad, it helps to talk to...

• After I've been mad, I feel...

• To prevent getting mad, I could..

Session 1

How Do I Feel?

Think about how you feel when you first start to get angry. Tick any of the following statements that apply to you.

I feel hot. ◯

My hands start to sweat. ◯

I find it difficult to stay still, I get fidgety. ◯

My mouth gets dry. ◯

My hands go into fists. ◯

My body feels tense. ◯

My heart races. ◯

I breathe more quickly. ◯

I feel panicky. ◯

Describe three more things that you might notice when you are beginning to get angry.

1. ....

....

2. ....

....

3. ....

....

The Assault Cycle

(from Coping with Aggressive Behaviour, Breakwell 1997)

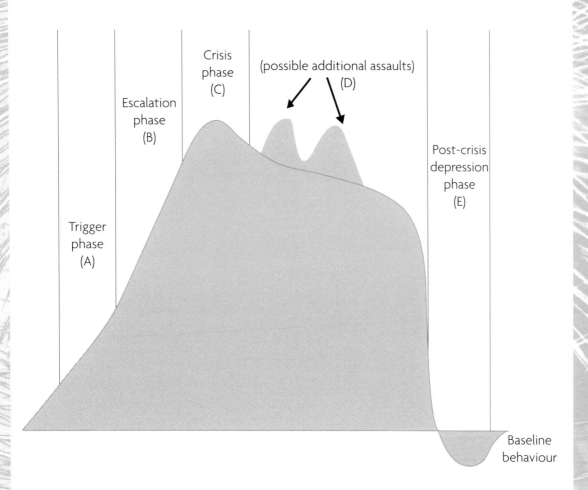

Keeping Calm

Dampening the fuse!

Here is a list of things that some people do in order to help them to calm down when they recognise the feelings that go along with being angry.

Choose three that you think might work for you and add any of your own that you have thought of or tried.

1.   Walking away from the incident.
2.   Counting to ten.
3.   Talking yourself into feeling calm.
4.   Using a catchphrase.
5.   Pretending to be somewhere else.
6.   Hiding behind an imaginary shield.
7.   Using the turtle technique and protecting yourself inside your shell.
8.   Taking some exercise – running, football, shooting baskets.
9.   Having a special place to go.
10.   Having a special person to be with.
11.   Listening to music.
12.   Breathing deeply and slowly.
13.   Relaxing clenched muscles.

The three that I think I will try are:

1. ....

2. ....

3. ....

Other things that I do to help me stay calm are ....

....

....

Take Home

My Strong Feelings Diary: Week 1

This coming week think about one strong feeling that you have had. Draw a picture of what gave you this strong feeling (trigger); circle the feeling you had (feeling); what you did (behaviour) and what happened next (consequences).

Then scale yourself on a scale of 1 – 10 for how well you coped with your strong feeling.

| 0 | 1 | 2 | 3 | 4 | 5 | 6 | 7 | 8 | 9 | 10 |

Not Well   OK   Brilliant

What made you have this strong feeling (trigger)?

What strong feeling did you have?

Was this feeling

Good

Neutral

Bad

What did you do (behaviour)?

What happened next (consequences)?

How well did you cope with your strong feeling?

/10

How could you have coped better with this strong feeling?

Session 1

Controlling Anger

Session 2
Fighting Friends

Resources to photocopy or print from the CD-ROM

Strong Feelings Diary Review: Week 1

Fighting Friends emotional story

Question Sheet

Top Tips for Josie

An Anger Model

My Anger Model

My Strong Feelings Diary: Week 2

Session 2: Fighting Friends

Aims of the session

- to focus on identifying solutions and alternatives to negative reactions
- to identify self-management strategies and methods which may impact positively on behaviours
- for pupils to be able to understand the anger model and begin to identify what triggers their own anger
- for pupils to draw up their own models for anger or strong feelings
- to set realistic goals and targets so as to reduce explosions and recognise and avoid triggers more successfully in the coming week.

Group session – 45 minutes to 1 hour

Circle warm-up – Angry balloon

This activity requires a balloon and a balloon pump. The aim is to provide pupils with a very visual representation of what occurs when anger is allowed to build up without access to a healthy method of calming and 'venting'. Pupils are asked to sit in a circle. The facilitator shows them the balloon and the pump and explains that between them they are going to tell the story of a boy called Alex who had difficulty controlling his anger.

The facilitator explains that he will begin the story and that each pupil will then contribute a sentence to continue the story, until everyone in the group has given a sentence outlining something that triggers Alex's feelings of anger. Each time a pupil offers a sentence towards the story and explains how Alex becomes angrier, the facilitator adds more air into the balloon.

The balloon represents Alex's build-up of anger and will demonstrate what eventually happens to a person if some of those feelings of anger are not 'vented' appropriately. The facilitator may wish to begin the story as follows:

> In a school not unlike our own there was a boy called Alex. Alex was a very angry boy (puff air into the balloon) who spent every waking hour of the day and night being and feeling angry (puff air into the balloon). Absolutely everything around him seemed to make him feel angry (puff air into the balloon). Things that you would have thought would brighten his day only seemed to contribute to his building feelings of anger; the sun shining made him feel angry (puff air into the balloon), being able to eat his lunch out on the school field with all his friends made him feel angry (puff air into the balloon), going on a school trip to Thorpe Park even made him feel angry (puff air into the balloon). It seemed that just getting out of bed in the mornings contributed to Alex's feelings of anger (puff air into the balloon). He just felt angry (puff air into the balloon), angry (puff air into the balloon), angry (puff air into the balloon) all day long.

The pupils then continues the story, providing examples of what makes Alex angry. When each pupil has said their angry sentence they pass the balloon and pump on to the next pupil after putting in a puff of air. This continues until the balloon bursts.

At this point the facilitator should emphasise that anger accumulates and without a suitable strategy to calm the feeling or 'vent' the frustration the smallest thing can 'trigger' the anger to explode. This explosion may often have far-reaching consequences.

Activity One – My strong feelings diary review

At the close of the previous session the strong feelings diary was introduced to the pupils. They were asked to complete it over the course of the previous week and to record an outburst of anger in terms of:

- Triggers – what made them angry, upset or stressed?
- Feelings – when they became angry, upset or stressed what feelings/reactions did they notice within themselves?
- Behaviour – what they did when they experienced an escalation of strong feelings
- Consequences – what happened next?

They were also asked to scale themselves on how well they coped with the escalation in strong feelings as marks out of 10.

| 0 | 5 | 10 |
| Not well | OK | Brilliant |

Within the Circle Time structure the facilitator now reviews the pupils' completed feelings diaries. Pupils are encouraged to share their successes and emotional triggers using the strong feelings diary review sheet. During this time it may be useful for pupils to discuss:

- triggers that caused them to become angry, upset or stressed
- what it felt like to be out of control
- what they did when they experienced an escalation of strong feelings
- what happened after they became angry, upset or out of control
- any successful calming strategies they used to de-escalate their strong feelings

Activity Two – Emotional story

Within the circle format the facilitator reads the emotional story to the group. This story describes how Josie becomes jealous of her best friend Zara, who has befriended a new pupil to the school; Shaheen. Even though Zara tries to include Josie in her games with Shaheen, Josie's feelings of jealousy become too much for her and she eventually accuses Zara of being a creep. After calling her best friend a creep, Josie spits into her face and runs away.

Activity Three – Question sheet

Pupils are then encouraged to analyse Josie's behaviour and the possible feelings/emotions that may have triggered her outbursts of angry behaviour. Through prompting by the facilitator pupils are asked a series of ten questions that are aimed at getting them to suggest strategies that could have been used by Josie to de-escalate her strong feelings of anger. These are as follows;

1. Why was Josie so fed up?

2. How did Zara feel when Josie shouted at her?

3. How do you think Shaheen felt when she heard Josie's comments?

4. How long had the two girls been best friends?

5. Why do you think Josie reacted so strongly?

6. What could Josie have done to prevent herself from being so unkind and getting so angry?

7. What advice would you give to Josie?

8. What do you think will happen next?

9. What is the best way to cope with jealousy?

10. How would you cope if you felt your best friend had let you down?

The pupils' responses can be recorded in note form by the facilitator using a whiteboard. This will take any stress out of the recording process and allow the pupils to focus on their thinking as opposed to worrying about recording responses on paper. It may be helpful to enlarge the question sheet to A3 size to act as a prompt and visual reminder to the children.

Activity Four – Top tips for Josie

Here the facilitator encourages pupils to reflect upon strategies that Josie could have used to help de-escalate her feelings before she reached the point of 'losing it'. Pupils can work through the format provided independently, recording their suggested strategies on the worksheet and then all answers can be drawn together during a Circle Time feed -back session. Using this method will of course be dependent upon the pupils' academic ability or willingness to put pen to paper; often pupils with behavioural difficulties may also experience learning difficulties. If this is not appropriate to the group or writing would cause the pupils to become unfocused or alienated do not pursue or insist on written answers, it would just make pupils unwilling to participate further in this session and future sessions. Gaining co-operative involvement is the key to success.

Consequently we would recommend that the facilitator act as a scribe for the pupils' ideas/ thoughts.

Alternatively, pupils may need to conduct this aspect of the session verbally within a Circle Time forum. This method requires a much more 'hands on' approach from the facilitator, who introduces the thoughtstorming format provided then models possible strategy suggestions for pupils. Once the facilitator has modelled one or two suggestions for possible strategies that Josie may have found useful, he or she needs to feed pupils an introductory sentence that they can then complete:

'Before losing control of his feelings Alex could have…'

Activity Five – An anger model

During this part of the session, pupils are introduced to a model of anger. This is shared with the pupils in order to provide them with a very clear visual image of how anger can manifest itself.

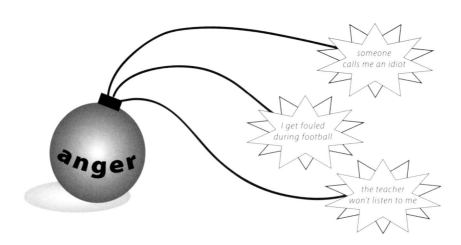

The facilitator explains that anger can be seen in term of a trigger, a fuse and an explosive bomb.

- A trigger – this is the match that ignites a person's fuse.
- A fuse – this is the mind reacting to the situation and can be viewed as thoughts/ feelings, e.g. threat or fear.
- The bomb/explosion – this is the body responding physiologically and may lead to anger being expressed.

Activity Six – My anger model

Having examined and discussed the model of anger (acting like a bomb), pupils are given the opportunity to design their own personal model of anger.

The facilitator may have to prompt pupils by asking them what they feel like when they get angry and finally 'lose it'. Pupils should be encouraged to develop an anger model that reflects their own behaviours, thoughts and feelings.

The pupils' own anger model can then be recorded on the activity sheet format provided. Remember there are no right and wrong models of their anger. Most important is the identification of a trigger, a fuse and an explosive device. Highlighting the necessity to include these key factors may be useful for pupils.

Plenary

The facilitator can prompt the pupils to review the session. It may be useful to focus on the following questions:

- What did you learn in this session?
- How do you feel about this session?
- How do you think this session might help you in the future?
- What advice would you give us if we ran this session again?

At the close of the session pupils are given another page of the strong feelings diary in the format provided, which they will be asked to complete over the course of the coming week.

This diary can then be reviewed in the next session within a Circle Time discussion.

Strong Feelings Diary Review: Week 1

Name:..

Date: ....

Last week my strong feeling was:

The feeling was:

☺	☺	☹
Good	Neutral	Bad

The trigger was:

My target for this week is:

I will watch out for these triggers:

•

•

•

I will try to cope with my strong feelings by thinking the following thoughts:

•

•

•

I will use the following strategies if I feel the EXPLOSION coming:

Signed: .... Date: ....

FIGHTING FRIENDS

Josie was in a really bad mood. As she walked to school she could feel herself getting angry and upset. It just wasn't fair. Why did Zara have to look after the new girl? Why couldn't Miss Hurt have asked someone else to do it? Why did she have to pick her best friend?

She kicked a stone along the pavement and turned the corner into the school playground. As she walked in Zara ran up to her. She was smiling. 'Come on Josie – play the skipping game with us,' she said. Josie looked at her friend and saw that the new girl was standing just behind her. She was going to join in with the game too. Josie suddenly felt her face flush red and clenched her fists. 'I don't want to play,' she said, staring straight at her friend. 'But why?' protested Zara looking confused. 'It's a great game and it will be nice to play with Shaheen. She's really nice and…'

'So what,' interrupted Josie. 'Just because you're creeping round her doesn't mean we all have to think she's so fantastic.' 'Josie – that's really nasty,' said Zara. She was genuinely shocked by Josie's behaviour. They had been best friends for 5 years – since they were in Year 2 and she'd never seen her act like this.

'I don't care what you think,' said Josie. 'Just go away and leave me alone. You're not my friend – you're just a stupid little creep and I don't ever want to talk to you again.'

Josie spat into Zara's face and then quickly turned and ran out of the playground and back into the street just as the bell for lessons was being rung.

Question Sheet

1. Why was Josie so fed up?

2. How did Zara feel when Josie shouted at her?

3. How do you think Shaheen felt when she heard Josie's comments?

4. How long had the two girls been best friends?

5. Why do you think Josie reacted so strongly?

6. What could Josie have done to prevent herself from being so unkind and getting so angry?

7. What advice would you give to Josie?

8. What do you think will happen next?

9. What is the best way to cope with jealousy?

10. How would you cope if you felt your best friend had let you down?

Top Tips for Josie

Problem Solve

Stop

Think

Reflect

What ideas do you have? How can Josie cope better? What strategies can she use? Record your ideas on this thoughtstorm sheet.

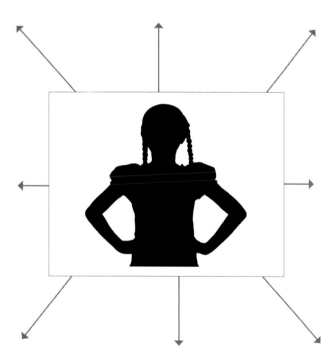

An Anger Model

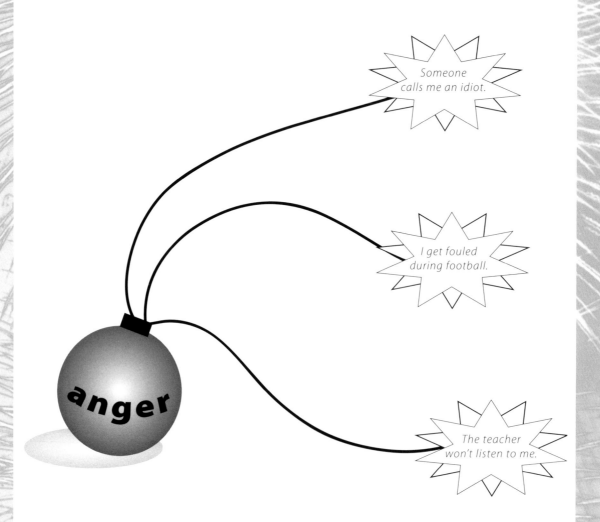

My Anger Model

Design your own anger model. Draw out what you think happens when you begin to feel angry, when you get very angry and when you finally lose it. Think of your own behaviour, thoughts and feelings. What image comes into your mind?

My Strong Feelings Diary: Week 2

This coming week think about one strong feeling that you have had. Draw a picture of what gave you this strong feeling (trigger); circle the feeling you had (feeling); what you did (behaviour) and what happened next (consequences).

Then scale yourself on a scale of 1 – 10 for how well you coped with your strong feeling.

| 0 | 1 | 2 | 3 | 4 | 5 | 6 | 7 | 8 | 9 | 10 |

Not Well   OK   Brilliant

What made you have this strong feeling (trigger)?

What strong feeling did you have?

Was this feeling

Good

Neutral

Bad

What did you do (behaviour)?

What happened next (consequences)?

How well did you cope with your strong feeling?

/10

How could you have coped better with this strong feeling?

Controlling Anger

Session 3
The Loss

Resources to photocopy or print from the CD-ROM

Strong Feelings Diary Review: Week 2

The Loss emotional story

Question Sheet

What Do I Think?

Strategy Sheet

Traffic Light Problem Solving Sheet

My Strong Feelings Diary: Week 3

Session 3: The Loss

Aims of the session

- to focus on identifying solutions and alternatives to negative reactions
- to identify self-management strategies and methods which may impact positively on behaviours
- for pupils to reflect upon incidents that have made them lose control and try to see them from a different perspective that does not incite their feelings of anger
- to introduce the traffic light strategy for recognising, analysing and implementing a stepped approach to controlling strong feelings
- to set realistic goals and targets so as to reduce explosions and recognise and avoid triggers more successfully in the coming week.

Group session – 45 minutes to 1 hour

Circle Warm-up – All change

The pupils should be seated in a circle ready to start the session. Pupils are then asked to change places in the circle if, for example:

- you like Chelsea football club
- you are wearing trainers
- you like playing cricket
- you hate eating fruit
- you love eating chocolate
- you like Cold Play.

This game can be continued to include any areas of significant interest to the pupils or possible common areas of dislike.

Activity One – My strong feelings diary review

At the close of the previous session the strong feelings diary was introduced to the pupils. They were asked to complete it over the course of the previous week and to record any outbursts of anger in terms of:

- Triggers – what made them angry, upset or stressed?
- Feelings – when they became angry, upset or stressed what feelings/reactions did they notice within themselves?
- Behaviour – what they did when they experienced an escalation of strong feelings.
- Consequences – what happened next?

3

They were also asked to scale themselves as to how well they coped with the escalation in strong feelings as marks out of 10.

| 0 | 5 | 10 |
| Not Well | OK | Brilliant |

Within the Circle Time structure the facilitator now reviews the pupils' completed feelings diary. Pupils are encouraged to share their successes and emotional triggers using the Strong Feelings Diary Review sheet. During this time it may be useful for pupils to discuss:

- triggers that caused them to become angry, upset or stressed
- what it felt like to be out of control
- what they did when they experienced an escalation of strong feelings
- what happened after they became angry, upset or out of control
- any successful calming strategies they used to de-escalate their strong feelings.

Activity Two – Emotional story

Within the circle the facilitator reads the emotional story to the group. This story describes how Amy's beloved Gran dies following a ten-month illness that ended in her having to be heavily sedated, to the extent that she did not even recognise her family members. Upon Amy's return to school, Amy's friends try to offer her support and provide a 'shoulder to cry on'. They keep trying to talk to her. Despite these attempts, Amy is feeling so lost and bereaved that she becomes angry at her friends and drives them away from her by swearing at them.

Activity Three – Question sheet

Pupils are then encouraged to analyse Amy's behaviour and emotional reactions. They are asked a series of ten questions which are aimed at prompting them to suggest why Amy said hurtful things to drive her friends away and what her friends thought about her behaviour. These are as follows:

1. Why did Amy feel so sad and so angry?

2. Why didn't she want a birthday party?

3. How did Amy feel when she went back to school?

4. How do you think her best friends felt when they first saw her?

5. Why did Amy get so angry with them?

6. What could she have done differently?

7. What could they have done differently?

8. Did the three girls do the 'right' thing by moving to another table?

9. How could Amy have stopped herself from getting so angry?

10. What do you think will happen next?

The pupil's responses can be recorded in note form by the facilitator using a whiteboard. This will take any stress out of the recording process and allow the children to focus on their thinking as opposed to worrying about recording. It may be helpful to enlarge the question sheet to A3 size to act as a prompt and visual reminder to the pupils.

Activity Four – What do I think?

Here the facilitator encourages pupils to reflect upon how commonly encountered situations can be viewed from different perspectives, which in turn affects the feelings associated with them. By working through the sheet the facilitator introduces the situation or 'trigger' and then encourages pupils to suggest how this may be interpreted as a fuse to their anger (creating angry feelings). The facilitator then encourages pupils to re-evaluate the situation from an alternative perspective that does not trigger such strong feelings. Pupils examine the following trigger situations:

- Someone pushes you in the playground.
- Your teacher doesn't listen when you are telling her why you are late.
- Your best friend does not talk to you.
- Someone takes your best ruler off your desk.
- You get told off for forgetting your homework.
- Someone shouts at you.
- A friend calls you a liar.
- You are not picked for the school football team.
- A group of children call you names as you walk past them.

This activity can be organised in one of two ways; pupils can work through the format provided independently, recording their suggested strategies on the worksheet and then all answers could be drawn together during a Circle Time feedback session.

Alternatively, pupils may need to conduct this aspect of the session verbally within a Circle Time forum. This method requires a much more 'hands on' approach from the facilitator, who introduces the thoughtstorming format provided, then models possible strategy suggestions for pupils. This takes away any stress involved in the recording process for pupils who have difficulties in this area. The facilitator should first model one or two possible strategies that he or she has found useful and should then feed pupils an introductory sentence that they can then complete:

'When my best friend does not speak to me I think he doesn't...' (strong feelings)

'When my best friend does not speak to me I think it is because she...' (gentle feelings)

Activity Five – Strategy sheet

During this part of the session, pupils are introduced to the traffic light system of identifying, analysing and implementing a strategy to de-escalate strong feelings.

This stepped approach is shared with the pupils in order to provide them with a very clear visual image of how strong feelings can be managed.

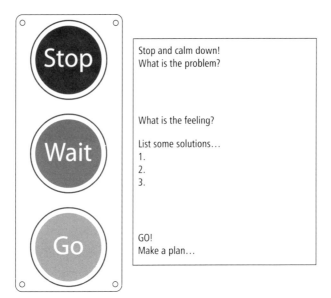

The facilitator explains that strong feelings can be managed in terms of: stopping, analysing what is wrong, identifying a suitable coping strategy and then putting it into action.

- Stop – identify what the problem is. This includes acknowledging what emotions are being experienced.

- Wait and plan – establish what should be done. Identify who could help and analyse the consequences of not de-escalating the strong feelings. Essentially design a plan to control them.

- Go – put the plan into action. If it fails, try again!

This sheet can be folded, laminated and then used as a bookmark for pupil's future use in class. It has worked most effectively when the class teacher has also been given a copy and actively models its appropriate use within the whole-class context. The use of this strategy for managing strong emotions could also be effectively adopted as a whole-class approach and fits well into the SEAL curriculum units.

Activity Six – Traffic lights problem-solving sheet

Having examined and discussed the traffic lights model of managing strong feelings, pupils are given the opportunity to utilise the traffic lights system to manage a fictional situation that would normally trigger these feelings. The facilitator may have to prompt pupils by asking them in what situations they get upset and finally 'lose it'. It may help to take one of the example trigger situations from the 'What do I think?' sheet used in Activity Four. Pupils should be encouraged to be reflective of how they realistically react to a trigger situation, identifying their own behaviour, thoughts and feelings. It would then be beneficial if pupils identified strategies and/or people who could help them to manage their strong feelings before they reached the point of being unable to control them.

Alternatively, pupils may need to conduct this aspect of the session verbally within a Circle Time forum. The facilitator introduces the thoughtstorming format provided and then models possible strategies for the students.

Plenary

The facilitator can prompt the pupils to review the session. It may be useful to focus on the following questions:

- What did you learn in this session?
- How do you feel about this session?
- How do you think this session might help you in the future?
- What advice would you give us if we ran this session again?

At the close of the session pupils are given another page of the strong feelings diary in the format provided, which they will be asked to complete over the course of the coming week.

This diary can then be reviewed in the next session within a Circle Time discussion.

Strong Feelings Diary Review: Week 2

Name:...

Date: ....

Last week my strong feeling was:

The feeling was:

Good   Neutral   Bad

The trigger was:

My target for this week is:

I will watch out for these triggers:

•

•

•

I will try to cope with my strong feelings by thinking the following thoughts:

•

•

•

I will use the following strategies if I feel the EXPLOSION coming:

Signed: .... Date: ....

Session 3

THE LOSS

Amy felt so sad and angry. Her Gran had died on Thursday night. It was awful. She had been ill for a long time – it seemed like years to Amy but ten months was a long time to someone who wasn't even ten years old yet. It was her tenth birthday next Tuesday but the last thing she felt like doing was celebrating and playing stupid games with stupid kids from school who didn't have a clue about what had been happening. She felt angry with everyone and angry about everything – especially with the fact that her lovely Gran had to be in such pain. No one seemed to be able to help her. They just kept giving her drugs to make her sleep. Towards the end, she didn't even know who they all were. It was terrible but it was also terrible now because Amy suddenly realised that she was never going to see her again. That was it. There was nothing anyone could do now.

When Amy went to school the following Monday she just felt an empty feeling in the pit of her stomach. She felt cold and numb inside. She just didn't want to talk to anyone – even her best friends Emily, Samantha and Chantelle.

They all sat next to her on her table and seemed to look embarrassed at first – like they didn't know what to say.

'Are you OK?' asked Emily.

'Can we do anything to help?' asked Samantha. 'Shall I ask Miss if we can work outside together?' asked Chantelle.

Amy just looked at them. 'You don't get it do you – you stupid jerks,' she said. 'I just don't want to be around any of you. You're all total idiots. I never liked you before my Gran died and now I just think you're a lot of losers so just clear off and leave me alone.' The three girls looked at each other in confusion. Then Samantha cleared her throat to speak. 'Look,' she said, 'we're only trying to help. There's no need to be so angry with us or to be nasty and unkind. After all, we're your mates aren't we?'

'You might have been but not now! I don't want to be anywhere near any of you so just piss off and leave me alone – now! Right now!' said Amy, her voice getting louder and more aggressive with every word. There was nothing else they could do. The three girls picked up their work and walked off to sit at another table.

Question Sheet

1. Why did Amy feel so sad and so angry?

2. Why didn't she want a birthday party?

3. How did Amy feel when she went back to school?

4. How do you think her best friends felt when they first saw her?

5. Why did Amy get so angry with them?

6. What could she have done differently?

7. What could they have done differently?

8. Did the three girls do the 'right' thing by moving to another table?

9. How could Amy have stopped herself from getting so angry?

10. What do you think will happen next?

What Do I Think?

Lengthening the fuse!

Trigger	What I think (strong feelings)	What I think (gentle feelings)
Someone pushes you in the playground.	1. He wants to pick a fight. 2. She wants to hurt me.	1. He lost his balance. 2. Someone bullied her into it.
Your teacher doesn't listen when you are telling them why you are late.	1. They don't care about me. 2. They don't believe me.	1. She is busy trying to sort out another problem. 2. I have picked a bad time. 3. I'm not making myself clear.
Your best friend does not talk to you.		
Someone takes your best ruler off your desk.		
You get told off for forgetting your homework.		
You are not picked for the school football team.		
A group of students call you names as you walk past them.		

Think about some incidents that have made you lose control recently and see if you can change what you think about them.

Strategy Sheet

Stop and calm down!
What is the problem?

What is the feeling?

List some solutions…
1.
2.
3.

GO!
Make a plan…

Traffic Lights Problem-Solving Sheet

Stop and Think

This is the problem ....

....

....

I feel ....

....

....

Wait and Plan

I should ....

....

The person who can help is ....

....

The consequences may include ....

....

....

GO!

I will try out this plan. If I do not succeed I will make a new plan and try again!

Signed: .... Date: ....

My Strong Feelings Diary: Week 3

This coming week think about one strong feeling that you have had. Draw a picture of what gave you this strong feeling (trigger); circle the feeling you had (feeling); what you did (behaviour) and what happened next (consequences).

Then scale yourself on a scale of 1 – 10 for how well you coped with your strong feeling.

0	1	2	3	4	5	6	7	8	9	10

Not Well   OK   Brilliant

What made you have this strong feeling (trigger)?

What strong feeling did you have?

Was this feeling

Good

Neutral

Bad

What did you do (behaviour)?

What happened next (consequences)?

How well did you cope with your strong feeling?

/10

How could you have coped better with this strong feeling?

Controlling Anger

Session 4
Cussing

Resources to photocopy or print from the CD-ROM

Strong Feelings Diary Review: Week 3

Cussing emotional story

Question Sheet

Early Warning Signs

Letting Off Steam

Change Your Thinking

My Strong Feelings Diary: Week 4

Session 4: Cussing

Aims of the session

- to focus on identifying solutions and alternatives to negative reactions
- to identify self-management strategies and methods which may impact positively on behaviours
- to identify/recognise the physical reactions to growing feelings of anger and stress
- to introduce the principle of 'letting off steam' as a strategy to de-escalate strong feelings
- to reinforce pupils' ability to reflect upon trigger situations and try and see them from a different perspective that does not incite such strong feelings
- to set realistic goals and targets so as to reduce explosions and recognise and avoid triggers more successfully in the coming week.

Group session — 45 minutes to 1 hour

Circle Warm-up — Pass the rhyme

The pupils should all be seated in a circle ready to start the session. In this warm-up the facilitator will need to explain that everyone in the circle is going to take a turn passing a particular rhythm around the circle. Once the rhythm has made one revolution of the group, a different person then creates a new rhythm to pass around the group. This continues until all the participants have had a turn at creating a rhythm for the group. Be prepared. Pupils love this activity and will often try to 'out do' each other in the creation of the most noise. You may wish to use some of the following ideas to get started:

- steady clapping
- clap hands and then stamp feet
- clicking fingers
- clap hands and then pat hands on knees
- click fingers and then tap shoulders.

The speed and pace of the rhythm can be increased or reduced to create quieter or noisier rhythms.

Activity One — My strong feelings diary review

At the close of the previous session the strong feelings diary was given to the pupils. They were asked to complete it over the course of the week and to record any outbursts of anger in terms of:

- Triggers – what made them angry, upset or stressed?

- Feelings – when they became angry, upset or stressed what feelings/reactions did they notice within themselves?

- Behaviour – what they did when they experienced an escalation of strong feelings.

- Consequences – what happened next?

They were also asked to scale themselves on how well they coped with the escalation in strong feelings as marks out of 10.

0	5	10
Not well	OK	Brilliant

Within the Circle Time structure the facilitator now reviews the pupils' completed feelings diaries. Pupils are encouraged to share their successes and emotional triggers using the strong feelings diary review sheet. During this time it may be useful for pupils to discuss:

- triggers that caused them to become angry, upset or stressed

- what it felt like to be out of control

- what they did when they experienced an escalation of strong feelings

- what happened after they became angry, upset or out of control

- any successful calming strategies they used to de-escalate their strong feelings.

Activity Two – Emotional story

Within the circle, the facilitator reads the emotional story to the group. This story describes how Jason's mother treated his whole class to a pool party for his birthday. The following Monday during an art class at school, Jason decides to make a thank-you card for his mother. While all his friends make comments about how generous his mum had been to throw the party for him, one of the girls comments that other people in the class just thought his mum was a 'show off'. The conversation between the two pupils descends into a verbal exchange of insults about their mothers. The exchange ultimately ends in Carmel slapping Jason across the face and then running out of the classroom.

Activity Three – Question sheet

Pupils are then encouraged to analyse Jason and Carmel's behaviour and the possible feelings and emotions that may have triggered their outbursts. They are asked a series of ten questions that are aimed at getting them to suggest what strategies could have been used by Jason and Carmel to de-escalate their strong feelings. These are as follows:

1. Why did Jason enjoy his party?

2. How was his mum generous to his classmates?

3. Why did Jason feel so proud?

4. How did Jason plan to thank his mum?

5. Why do you think that Carmel was so unkind to Jason? What do you think of her behaviour?

6. Why did Jason cuss Carmel's mum?

7. What could Jason have done/said differently?

8. What advice would you give to Jason now?

9. What advice would you give to Carmel now?

10. What do you think will happen next?

The pupils' responses can be recorded in note form by the facilitator using a whiteboard. This will take any stress out of the recording process and allow the pupils to focus on their thinking as opposed to worrying about recording responses on paper. It may be helpful to enlarge the question sheet to A3 size to act as a prompt and visual reminder to the pupils.

Activity Four – Early warning signs

Here the facilitator encourages pupils to reflect upon how a person reacts physically to growing feelings of distress. They are asked to examine a tick sheet detailing the physical signs associated with feelings of anger and stress and try to relate them to their own personal experience. This activity is best completed on an individual basis. However, if necessary the facilitator can act as scribe for the group, with the majority of the task being conducted verbally within a Circle Time forum.

Activity Five – Letting off steam strategy sheet

During this part of the session, the pupils are introduced to the letting off steam strategy to de-escalate strong feelings. This is shared with the pupils in order to provide them with a very practical method as to how strong feelings can be managed. The facilitator explains that such feelings can be managed in terms of the following process:

1. Breathe in deeply.

2. Count to 20 – slowly.

3. Let out your breath and feel your tensions being zapped!

After discussing how pupils might practically use the letting off steam strategy, pupils can then create their own poster on the format provided to illustrate how they could use this strategy. There are no 'right' or 'wrong' pictures. These are very much a personal representation of the pupils' own feelings. If time allows, pupils may wish to colour their posters.

Activity Six – Change your thinking

This activity is aimed at reinforcing the previous session's work on encouraging pupils to become more reflective and take into account the feelings and reactions of those around them. It is important for them to acknowledge that the behaviour of others (that may prove to be a 'trigger' for their strong feelings) may have a complex root cause that is personally unrelated to the pupil.

Pupils should be encouraged to be reflective about how they realistically react to a trigger situation, identifying their own behaviours, thoughts and feelings. It would then be beneficial if they could identify strategies and/or people who could help them to manage their strong feelings before they reached the point of being unable to control them.

This activity can be organised in one of two ways: pupils can work through the format provided independently, recording their suggested strategies on the activity sheet, and then all answers could be drawn together during a Circle Time feedback session. Alternatively, the facilitator can act as a scribe for all the pupils' ideas, drawing these together on a whiteboard.

Plenary

The facilitator can prompt the pupils to review the session. It may be useful to focus on the following questions:

- What did you learn this session?
- How do you feel about this session?
- How do you think this session might help you in the future?
- What advice would you give us if we ran this session again?

At the close of the session pupils are given another page of the strong feelings diary in the format provided, which they will be asked to complete over the course of the coming week.

This anger can then be reviewed in the next session within a Circle Time discussion.

Strong Feelings Diary Review: Week 3

Name: ....

Date: ....

Last week my strong feeling was:

The feeling was:

Good   Neutral   Bad

The trigger was:

My target for this week is:

I will watch out for these triggers:

-
-
-

I will try to cope with my strong feelings by thinking the following thoughts:

-
-
-

I will use the following strategies if I feel the EXPLOSION coming:

Signed: .... Date: ....

CUSSING

Jason really enjoyed his birthday party. His mum had been really kind and treated his whole class to a pool party. No one had been left out and even Mr Price, his teacher, had been invited. He couldn't come because it was the Friday night when he was doing a coaching course at the local gym but everyone else was there and had a brilliant time. The food was really good and his mum got everyone a special present to take home.

'Your mum's just so kind', said Anna when they got to school the following Monday.

'That party was the best one I've ever been to,' said Michael. 'Your mum is dead generous.' Jason smiled. He felt really proud. It was nice to have such a lovely mum. He decided to make her a special card in the Art lesson that afternoon to say thank you.

After lunch Mr Price set up the classroom for the Art lesson. Everyone was allowed to have free choice, which meant they could choose to do anything from watercolours and still lifes to colouring mosaic patterns with fine felt tips. Jason sat at the craft table and began to cut out petals for the flower at the front of the card. He sat next to Carmel. She was making a card for her sister's birthday.

'What are you making?' she asked him. 'It's a special thank you card for my mum', he said. 'She was so kind last week. She gave me the best birthday party ever... everyone said so and they all said she was the best mum ever,' he beamed.

Carmel screwed up her nose and sneered. 'No they didn't – not everyone. Some of us just thought she was a bit of a show off.' Jason looked shocked. 'What do you mean? She's not. She's the best – not like your Mum.' 'What are you saying?' said Carmel looking flushed. 'Your Mum's just a big fat slob – everyone says so. She's a big fat cow who couldn't even afford a party – even a small one because she's on benefits. She's just a fat scrounger.'

Carmel saw red. She stood up and slapped Jason around the head before running out of the classroom with tears streaming down her face.

Question Sheet

1. Why did Jason enjoy his party?

2. How was his mum generous to his classmates?

3. Why did Jason feel so proud?

4. How did Jason plan to thank his mum?

5. Why do you think that Carmel was so unkind to Jason? What do you think of her behaviour?

6. Why did Jason cuss Carmel's mum?

7. What could Jason have done/said differently?

8. What advice would you give to Jason now?

9. What advice would you give to Carmel now?

10. What do you think will happen next?

Early Warning Signs

Listen, look and feel!

Things that happen to me when I begin to feel angry or stressed:

	Yes	Sometimes	No
Begin to feel hot/cold	◯	◯	◯
Sweat	◯	◯	◯
Dry throat/mouth	◯	◯	◯
Tension in neck, shoulders, back	◯	◯	◯
Feel a change in facial colour	◯	◯	◯
Eye contact: avoid contact/start to stare	◯	◯	◯
Start to fidget	◯	◯	◯
Start to move/talk more quickly	◯	◯	◯
Start to handle equipment heavily/thump things down	◯	◯	◯
Start to put hands on hips/fold arms	◯	◯	◯
Notice a change in proximity to other people (too close/avoid proximity/other)	◯	◯	◯
Change in body posture	◯	◯	◯
Use of defensive gestures	◯	◯	◯
Change in breathing	◯	◯	◯
Heart starts to palpitate	◯	◯	◯
Feel pulse racing	◯	◯	◯
Experience headache/other pain	◯	◯	◯
Jaw becomes tight	◯	◯	◯
Change in tone of voice	◯	◯	◯
Change in pitch of voice	◯	◯	◯
Change in delivery of words and/or sentences	◯	◯	◯
Stuttering/difficulty with formulating sentences	◯	◯	◯
Use of sarcastic/unkind remarks	◯	◯	◯
Use of mild threats	◯	◯	◯
Other	◯	◯	◯

Session 4

Letting Off Steam

Strategy sheet

Don't explode! Take a deep breath and slowly let off the steam!

Practise your skills:

1. Breathe in deeply.
2. Count to 20 – slowly.
3. Let out your breath and feel your anger being zapped!

Design your own poster in the frame, using the title: 'Letting Off Steam'.

4

Change Your Thinking!

You know your triggers – now change how you think about them.

Create a new script.

	The trigger	What I think and do	What I could think and do
1.			
2.			
3.			
4.			

My Strong Feelings Diary: Week 4

This coming week think about one strong feeling that you have had. Draw a picture of what gave you this strong feeling (trigger); circle the feeling you had (feeling); what you did (behaviour) and what happened next (consequences).

Then scale yourself on a scale of 1 – 10 for how well you coped with your strong feeling.

| 0 | 1 | 2 | 3 | 4 | 5 | 6 | 7 | 8 | 9 | 10 |

Not Well   OK   Brilliant

What made you have this strong feeling (trigger)?

What strong feeling did you have?
Was this feeling

Good

Neutral

Bad

What did you do (behaviour)?

What happened next (consequences)?

How well did you cope with your strong feeling?

/10

How could you have coped better with this strong feeling?

Session 4

Controlling Anger

Session 5
Feeling Stupid

Resources to photocopy or print from the CD-ROM

Strong Feelings Diary Review: Week 4

Feeling Stupid emotional story

Question Sheet

Time-out Strategy Sheet

Problem Cards

Problem Solving Framework

My Strong Feelings Diary: Week 5

Session 5: Feeling Stupid

Aims of the session

- to focus on identifying solutions and alternatives to negative reactions
- to identify self-management strategies and methods which may impact positively on behaviours
- to identify/recognise the physical reactions to strong feelings
- to introduce the principle of time out as a strategy to de-escalate strong feelings
- to reinforce pupils' ability to reflect upon trigger situations and try to use the traffic lights strategy for recognising, analysing and implementing a stepped approach to controlling feelings of anger.

Group session – 45 minutes to 1 hour

Circle Warm-up – Wink wink

Pupils need to be seated on chairs in a circle. An additional chair should have been placed into the circle prior to the pupils entering the room. Once the pupils are all seated, the pupil seated next to the empty chair is asked to wink at someone in the circle who is seated on the other side of the circle. The pupil who has been winked at then has to cross the circle in silence and sit on the empty chair. The person who now has the empty chair on their right is required to take up the winking role and needs to wink at someone else across the circle. Once again the pupil who has been winked at needs to cross the circle in silence and sit in the vacant chair. This continues until all the pupils have been mixed up in their seating. The real fun in the game comes with ensuring that the pace of the winking and the subsequent pupils' movement between chairs is as fast as possible.

Activity One – My strong feelings diary review

At the close of the previous session the strong feelings diary sheet was provided to the pupils. They were asked to complete it over the course of the week and to record any outbursts of anger in terms of:

- Triggers – what made them angry, upset or stressed?
- Feelings – when they became angry, upset or stressed what feelings/reactions did they notice within themselves?
- Behaviour – what they did when they experienced an escalation of strong feelings.
- Consequences – what happened next?

They were also asked to scale themselves on how well they coped with the escalation in strong feelings as marks out of 10.

0   5   10

Not well   OK   Brilliant

Within the Circle Time structure the facilitator now reviews the pupils' completed feelings diaries. Pupils are encouraged to share their successes and emotional triggers using the strong feelings diary review sheet. During this time it may be useful for pupils to discuss:

- Triggers that caused them to become angry, upset or stressed
- What it felt like to be out of control
- What they did when they experienced an escalation of strong feelings
- What happened after they became angry, upset or out of control
- Any successful calming strategies they used to de-escalate their strong feelings.

Activity Two – Emotional story

Within the circle, the facilitator reads the emotional story to the group. This story describes how Henry experiences significant difficulties with his literacy work. He is well aware that the other members of his class are achieving at a higher level than he is. Henry's class teacher is kind and understanding and has worked hard with him to help him improve his reading. Unfortunately, his teacher leaves the school to return home to Australia to be with her sick mother. The new supply teacher asks Henry to pluralise a word and spell it in front of the whole class. When Henry is unable to do this another pupil in the class tells the teacher that he cannot do the work because he is special needs and the class dunce. As a result of the high level of frustration and upset that he experiences at this humiliation in front of his whole class, Henry starts a fight with the boy right in front of the teacher.

Activity Three – Question sheet

Pupils are then encouraged to analyse Henry's behaviour and the possible feelings and emotions that may have triggered his outbursts. Pupils are asked a series of ten questions that are aimed at encouraging them to suggest what strategies could have been used by Henry to de-escalate his strong feelings. These are as follows:

1. Why did Henry hate writing?
2. How did his difficulties make him feel?
3. How would you feel if you were in his shoes?
4. Why was his mum pleased with his teacher?
5. Why did his teacher have to leave the school so suddenly?
6. Do you think the supply teacher meant to embarrass Henry?
7. What do you think of Alex's comments?
8. Why did Henry 'lose it'?

9. What could he have done differently?

10. What do you think will happen next?

The pupils' responses can be recorded in note form by the facilitator using a whiteboard. This will take any stress out of the recording process and allow for a focus on thinking as opposed to worrying about recording responses on paper. It may be helpful to enlarge the question sheet to A3 size to act as a prompt and visual reminder to the pupils.

Activity Four – Time out strategy sheet

In this activity the facilitator encourages pupils to reflect upon how they physically look when they are experiencing strong feelings. It may be useful to practise making angry faces or distressed faces and allow pupils to look at themselves in a mirror. It is advisable to have one big mirror rather than let pupils to have their own individual mirrors, as they can be extremely distracting! The pupils can record these faces on the format provided. Alternatively the facilitator could take digital photos of the pupils making an angry or distressed face. These could then be printed off and glued onto the format.

This activity also provides the facilitator with the opportunity to reinforce how pupils can use their skills to identify the physical reactions of growing anger (as a precursor to an outburst of inappropriate behaviour), which allows pupils to take a 'step back'. They can then implement a calming strategy that is aimed at de-escalating these uncomfortable feelings. Pupils work through the format provided and record calming strategies that they could use. Although this is best completed on an individual basis the facilitator can, if necessary, act as scribe for the group, with the majority of the task being conducted verbally within a Circle Time context. It may be useful to draw the pupils' attention to the following de-escalation strategies;

- taking deep breaths;

- having a time out

- talking to another person/friend/adult

- counting

- splashing water on their face

- using the traffic light strategy (covered in a previous session)

Activity Five – Problem cards

This activity is aimed at reinforcing the previous session's work on encouraging pupils to become more reflective and to also take into account the feelings and reactions of those around them. It is important for pupils to acknowledge that the behaviour of others (that may prove to be a 'trigger' for their outbursts) may have a complex root cause that is personally unrelated to the pupil.

The facilitator will need to make up the problem cards from the format provided. We suggest that this activity is organised in the following way: Firstly, place the problem cards face down on the table and ask the pupils to select one each. They can then examine the difficulty described on the card in terms of:

1. Identifying what the problem is.

2. Identifying the feelings that are associated with the trigger situations.

3. Using the stop, think and make a plan traffic light system to resolve/control their feelings in the given situation.

4. Reflecting upon identifying key indicators that demonstrate to pupils when a problem has been solved.

Pupils can then record their thoughts, ideas and strategies on the format provided. All answers could then be drawn together during a Circle Time feedback session. If recording is an issue for some pupils, then feedback can be given orally as part of a circle discussion. Once again, this will reduce any stress and encourage participation.

Plenary

The facilitator can prompt the pupils to review the session. It may be useful to focus on the following questions:

- What did you learn this session?

- How do you feel about this session?

- How do you think this session might help you in the future?

- What advice would you give us if we ran this session again?

At the close of the session pupils are given another page of the strong feelings diary on the format provided, which they will be asked to complete over the course of the coming week.

This diary can then be reviewed in the next session within a Circle Time discussion.

Strong Feelings Diary Review: Week 4

Name: ....

Date: ....

Last week my strong feeling was:

The feeling was:

Good   Neutral   Bad

The trigger was:

My target for this week is:

I will watch out for these triggers:

-
-
-

I will try to cope with my strong feelings by thinking the following thoughts:

-
-
-

I will use the following strategies if I feel the EXPLOSION coming:

Signed: .... Date: ....

FEELING STUPID

Henry really hated writing. He tried really, really hard but he just didn't seem to get the hang of it. He just couldn't remember which way round the letters went and always confused his b's and d's. He felt so stupid. He couldn't even remember simple words like 'today' or 'went' or 'bed'. His teacher had been really kind though and tried to help him with lots of different activities. She got him to put the words together with plastic letters and used different colours to show him the patterns in groups of words. She also made sure that he never had to read out loud in front of the class and she made him special activity sheets so that he could get on with his work when the rest of the class were doing Literacy Hour. His mum was really pleased and said that she didn't think there were many teachers who worked as hard or cared so much. She said that if he carried on trying, then he was bound to make progress soon. Henry wasn't so sure. He knew how hard he found the work – even though it was designed especially for him. Also, he knew how far ahead all the others in his class were. No one had his problem. They could all read and write and spell as if it was a piece of cake. It just wasn't fair.

Then, his teacher left the school. It happened really suddenly. She had a phone call on the Friday to say that her mum had been diagnosed with cancer. She only had a few months to live so Miss Jeffries had to go straight back to Australia. Everyone in Henry's class was upset. They had all liked her and now they were going to have a supply teacher. Henry felt sick when he went into the classroom that Monday. How was he going to cope? What if the new teacher didn't understand?

As he walked into class, he could feel his heart beating really fast. Mr Michaels stood at the front of the class and smiled. He introduced himself and then asked all the children to get out their Literacy books.

'We're going to do plurals today,' he beamed. Henry shuddered.

'Now – who can tell me the plural of lolly and how to spell it?' he asked and then pointed straight at Henry. Henry gulped. He heard two people giggling behind him. He just stared at Mr Michaels who began to look a bit concerned.

'Come on – don't be shy,' he said.

'He's not shy, Sir' said Alex. 'He's just stupid like the class dunce – he's got special needs.'

Mr Michaels looked embarrassed and went to turn once again to Henry but it was too late. Henry had lost it. He jumped on Alex before Mr Michaels could do anything to stop him.

Question Sheet

1. Why did Henry hate writing?

2. How did his difficulties make him feel?

3. How would you feel if you were in his shoes?

4. Why was his mum pleased with his teacher?

5. Why did his teacher have to leave the school so suddenly?

6. Do you think the supply teacher meant to embarrass Henry?

7. What do you think of Alex's comments?

8. Why did Henry 'lose it'?

9. What could he have done differently?

10. What do you think will happen next?

Time-out Strategy Sheet

Draw yourself outside a door feeling upset, angry or stressed. Show on your picture how you look when you feel such strong feelings.

How will you calm yourself down? Make a list of things you can do, say to yourself and think about.

- Do: ....

   ....

- Say to yourself: ....

   ....

- Think about: ....

   ....

Problem Cards

Jason is hurt and upset because his dad keeps calling him 'Dumbo' as he finds school work difficult.	**Emma is stressed** because her mum and dad are splitting up as her dad has got a new girlfriend.	**Mr Jones is furious** because the children in his class were so poorly behaved on the trip to Thorpe Park.
Mrs Jarvis is mad because the next door neighbours' dog keeps fouling at her gate.	**John is really jealous** because his mum has had a new baby and she's got no time for him now.	**Mel is hurt and left out** because she has not been picked for the school football team.
Mr Charlston is totally fed-up because his wife is always nagging him about doing jobs around the house after work when he is tired.	**Shakira is distressed** because her best friend has gone off with a new girl and she feels left out.	**Jamil is intimidated and hurt** because two boys in his class keep saying that he is a terrorist because he's Muslim.
Charlie is in agony because his nan is ill with cancer and she is going to die soon.	**Adil is really upset** because his mum won't let him go on the school trip with the rest of the class.	**Sara is jealous, hurt and upset** because she can't do the spellings like the other children in her class and she feels stupid.

Problem Solving Framework

- What is the problem?

- What are the feelings?

- Stop and think and make a plan.

What can they do?

How can they think differently?

Who can help them?

- TRY IT OUT! How will they know when the problem has been solved?

- What will be different?

Thank you for your help!

My Strong Feelings Diary: Week 5

This coming week think about one strong feeling that you have had. Draw a picture of what gave you this strong feeling (trigger); circle the feeling you had (feeling); what you did (behaviour) and what happened next (consequences).

Then scale yourself on a scale of 1 – 10 for how well you coped with your strong feeling.

Not Well   OK   Brilliant

What made you have this strong feeling (trigger)?

What strong feeling did you have?

Was this feeling

Good   Neutral   Bad

What did you do (behaviour)?

What happened next (consequences)?

How well did you cope with your strong feeling?

/10

How could you have coped better with this strong feeling?

Session 5

Controlling Anger

Session 6
The Foul

Resources to photocopy or print from the CD-ROM

Strong Feelings Diary Review: Week 5

The Foul emotional story

Question Sheet

Using 'I' Messages Strategy Sheet

Talk Time Strategy Sheet

Problem Solving Sheet

My Strong Feelings Diary: Week 6

Session 6: The Foul

Aims of the session

- to focus on identifying solutions and alternatives to negative reactions

- to introduce the 'I' message strategy for examining a 'trigger' situation and suggesting possible solutions

- to identify self-management strategies and methods which may impact positively on behaviours

- to identify/recognise the physical reactions to strong feelings

- to introduce the principle of time-out as a strategy to de-escalate uncomfortable feelings

- to reinforce pupils' ability to reflect upon trigger situations and try to use the traffic light strategy for recognising, analysing and implementing a stepped approach to controlling strong feelings.

Group session – 45 minutes to 1 hour

Circle Warm-up – The compliment game

Within the circle, pupils take it in turns to call out the name of another member of the group and then say something positive about them. As they call out the person's name and their compliment, they mime throwing them a ball. The pupil whose name has been called then reaches out to 'catch' the imaginary ball. Once they have caught the ball they then call out the name of another pupil and a compliment about them while also miming throwing them a 'ball'. This process continues until everyone in the group has had an opportunity to have a turn. Throughout a game such as this, pupils often end up passing the 'ball' to somebody they do not usually associate with. By offering a compliment, it also allows them to try to focus on more positive aspects of each other rather than on the negatives. The facilitator may need to model the use of compliments to the pupils as they can find expressing and accepting positive comments about themselves difficult. The following compliment ideas may help to get the game started. The names will need to reflect the pupils within the group!

- Joe is good at football.

- Hamza walked away from an argument this week.

- Ellie has nice handwriting.

- Sam always says thank you when he is given something.

- Ryan is good at D.T.

- Nicky dances really well.

- Mary is brilliant on the computer.

If the group are suitably receptive and able to cope with the use of equipment without the situation becoming too uncontrolled, the facilitator can re-run the game, giving pupils a soft ball to throw as they offer each other compliments.

Activity One – My strong feelings diary review

At the close of the previous session the strong feelings diary was given to the pupils. They were asked to complete it over the course of the previous week and to record any outbursts of anger in terms of:

- Triggers – what made them angry, upset or stressed?

- Feelings – when they became angry, upset or stressed what feelings/reactions did they notice within themselves?

- Behaviour – what they did when they experienced an escalation of strong feelings.

- Consequences – what happened next?

They were also asked to scale themselves on how well they coped with the escalation in strong feelings as marks out of 10.

0	5	10
Not well	OK	Brilliant

Within the Circle Time structure the facilitator now reviews the pupils' completed feelings diaries. Pupils are encouraged to share their successes and emotional triggers using the strong feelings diary review sheet. During this time it may be useful for pupils to discuss:

- triggers that caused them to become angry, upset or stressed

- what it felt like to be out of control

- what they did when they experienced an escalation of strong feelings

- what happened after they became angry, upset or out of control

- any successful calming strategies they used to de-escalate their strong feelings

Activity Two – Emotional story

Within the circle the facilitator reads the emotional story to the group. This story details how talent scouts from a regional football team come to watch Caris, who is a gifted footballer. During the match, Caris is verbally tormented by an opposition player and then deliberately kicked in the back. Unfortunately the referee fails to notice the foul and the girl gets away with it. This causes Caris to lose her temper and she chases the other player and thumps her in the back.

Activity Three – Question sheet

Pupils are then encouraged to analyse Caris's behaviour and the possible feelings and emotions that may have triggered her outbursts. They are asked a series of ten questions which are aimed at encouraging them to suggest what strategies could have been used by Caris to de-escalate her strong feelings. These are as follows:

1. Why did Caris love playing football?

2. Why was she labelled a 'tomboy'?

3. How did her dad feel about her football skills?

4. Why was Caris so excited about this match?

5. Why do you think the other player called Caris a loser?

6. Why was it so important for Caris to keep her temper?

7. How was Caris fouled?

8. Why did Caris feel so angry?

9. What could she have done differently?

10. What do you think will happen next?

The pupils' responses can be recorded in note form by the facilitator using a whiteboard. This will take any stress out of the recording process and allow for a focus on thinking as opposed to worrying about recording responses on paper. It may be helpful to enlarge the question sheet to A3 size to act as a prompt and visual reminder.

Activity Four – Using 'I' messages strategy sheet

Here the facilitator encourages pupils to reflect upon the problem of Michael, who hits out and hurts Jason because he fouled him during a game of football. The class teacher is very upset with Michael and calls his mum into school. The pupils are asked what Michael could have done differently. This presents them with an opportunity to use their reflective skills to analyse what would be appropriate behaviour in a potential 'trigger' situation. To reinforce and continue the development of pupils' empathy levels, they are then asked to place themselves in Michael's 'shoes' and record an 'I' message from him to his victim Jason. This provides the pupils with the opportunity to examine a common 'trigger' situation with a greater degree of objectivity. The facilitator may need to model the use of 'I' messages to the pupils. The following 'I' messages may prove useful as a starting point:

- I don't like the way you fouled me.

- I could have been seriously injured by that foul.

- I don't think it's good sportsmanship to foul people like that.

- I think that if you carry on playing like that someone will get really hurt.

- I think that it would be better if you weren't so aggressive in getting the ball.

The facilitator then works with the pupils through the format provided and records 'I' messages for the discussed problem. This can then lead into a discussion in which pupils can share a problem from their own experience.

Activity Five – Talk time strategy sheet

This activity is aimed at encouraging pupils to consider using the talk time strategy to help resolve/de-escalate their strong feelings.

The facilitator should highlight the fact that sometimes it helps to share a problem with a friend, thereby allowing them to offer possible suggestions that could resolve the situation and the difficult feelings associated with it. In pairs, the pupils are asked to interview each other and find the best solution to a problem they currently have or have previously experienced. Using the format provided, they are encouraged to work through the following questions:

- What is the problem?
- How do you feel?
- What do you want to happen?
- What do you need to do to change things?
- Does anyone/anything else need to change?
- What can you do differently?

Pupils can record their thoughts, ideas and strategies on the format provided. All answers could then be drawn together by the facilitator during a Circle Time feedback session. If students have difficulties in recording, then feedback can be given verbally in a circle discussion.

Activity Six – Problem solving sheet

This activity encourages pupils to become more reflective regarding their own behaviour. It would help if the facilitator supports the pupils in focusing upon a particular problem that regularly occurs. The specific 'trigger' situation or problem may vary between pupils within the group. By working through this worksheet format, pupils can identify:

- the root of the problem
- the feelings involved when the problem occurs
- what they would like to happen
- what they need to change in order to facilitate the solution they envisage
- what those around them could change to help them attain their goal
- how they would feel if the suggested changes are implemented
- how the suggested changes will assist them in resolving their problem.

By reflecting upon all the above areas, pupils can then identify the root of their difficulty and begin to develop an appropriate method by which they can tackle and resolve the problem without incurring a build-up of uncontrollable feelings.

Within the circle the facilitator can then draw all the suggestions together and offer an opportunity to share ideas.

Plenary

The facilitator can then prompt the pupils to review the session. It may be useful to focus on the following questions:

- What did you learn this session?

- How do you feel about this session?

- How do you think this session might help you in the future?

- What advice would you give us if we ran this session again?

At the close of the session pupils are given another page of the strong feelings diary in the format provided, which they will be asked to complete over the course of the coming week.

This diary can then be reviewed in the next session within a Circle Time discussion.

6

Strong Feelings Diary Review: Week 5

Name:..

Date: ....

Last week my strong feeling was:

The feeling was:

Good   Neutral   Bad

The trigger was:

My target for this week is:

I will watch out for these triggers:

•

•

•

I will try to cope with my strong feelings by thinking the following thoughts:

•

•

•

I will use the following strategies if I feel the EXPLOSION coming:

Signed: .... Date: ....

THE FOUL

Caris loved playing football. She had always been labelled a 'tomboy' by the other girls in her class but she didn't care. As far as she was concerned, they were all soft and would never understand how she felt about the game. She wasn't interested in the newest fashions or girls' games (as she called them). She simply wanted to be the best footballer in the school and to get into the Girls' England squad. Her Dad was really proud of her. There was a big match coming up this Saturday and he was particularly excited because two talent scouts were coming to observe the players. There was a real chance that Caris could be picked for the Regional Girls' Team.

When the big day arrived, Caris was feeling really nervous. She knew exactly how important it was to play her very best. She also knew that her team would have some stiff opposition from Cherry Lane Girls as they had some good players and an excellent goalie. Then the referee blew the whistle, and before she knew it the match was on.

Caris immediately took hold of the ball. Then she was tackled by a tall blonde girl who successfully got the ball from her and moved on towards the goal. As she did so, she smirked at Caris and said under her breath, 'No chance, you little loser.' Caris felt angry but she knew she couldn't show it. There was no way a talent scout would want someone who couldn't keep their temper in a Regional team. She bit her lip and carried on with the game. Ten minutes later, she found herself once again with the ball and just knew she could score – if only she could get past the tall blonde girl. She dribbled the ball straight towards her and before she could strike it, the blonde player kicked her in the back from behind so hard that Caris doubled over – totally winded.

'Foul!' shouted her dad from the touchline but no one else seemed to have seen this – including the referee. Caris was astonished and then she suddenly felt really angry. That may have been her one big chance. She felt hot and determined to get her own back. She ran after the blonde player and thumped her hard from behind. Immediately the referee blew his whistle. She was being sent off! 'It's not fair!' she shouted but it was too late now.

6

Question Sheet

1. Why did Caris love playing football?

2. Why was she labelled a 'tomboy'?

3. How did her dad feel about her football skills?

4. Why was Caris so excited about this match?

5. Why do you think the other player called Caris a loser?

6. Why was it so important for Caris to keep her temper?

7. How was Caris fouled?

8. Why did Caris feel so angry?

9. What could she have done differently?

10. What do you think will happen next?

Using 'I' Messages Strategy Sheet

A Problem

Michael hit out and hurt Jason because he fouled him in the football game. The teacher was upset and called his mum into school.

What could Michael have done differently?

....

....

....

Write down an 'I' message for Michael to give to Jason.

'I...

....

'

Make up your own 'I' message for this problem.

'I...

....

....

Make up your own 'I' message for your own problem.

'I...

....

....

Don't forget to use them!

Talk Time Strategy Sheet

Tell a friend!

Share the problem!

Sometimes it helps to talk to a friend.

Use the following questions to interview each other and find out the best solution.

- What is the problem?

- How do you feel?

- What do you want to happen?

- What do you need to do to change things?

- Does anyone/anything else need to change?

- What can you do differently?

Let's make a plan! If it doesn't work, we'll try again.

Good luck!

Problem Solving Sheet

My problem is:

• ....

• ....

My feelings now are:

• ....

• ....

I would like this to happen:

....

....

In order to CHANGE things I need to do these things:

• ....

• ....

Other people can also help by changing these things:

• ....

• ....

If these changes are made I will feel...

happy/excited   annoyed/irritated   angry/stressed frustrated

If these changes are made, I will be able to sort out this problem because:

• ....

• ....

My Strong Feelings Diary: Week 6

This coming week think about one strong feeling that you have had. Draw a picture of what gave you this strong feeling (trigger); circle the feeling you had (feeling); what you did (behaviour) and what happened next (consequences).

Then scale yourself on a scale of 1 – 10 for how well you coped with your strong feeling.

0	1	2	3	4	5	6	7	8	9	10

Not Well   OK   Brilliant

What made you have this strong feeling (trigger)?

What strong feeling did you have?

Was this feeling

Good

Neutral

Bad

What did you do (behaviour)?

What happened next (consequences)?

How well did you cope with your strong feeling?

/10

How could you have coped better with this strong feeling?

Controlling Anger

Session 7
Bully Boys

Resources to photocopy or print from the CD-ROM

Strong Feelings Diary Review: Week 6

Bully Boys emotional story

Question Sheet

What Makes Me Lose It?

Bully Box

Anger Strategy Sheet

My Strong Feelings Diary: Week 7

Session 7: Bully Boys

Aims of the session

- to focus on identifying solutions and alternatives to negative reactions

- to introduce the use of 'physical' strategies for working through strong feelings

- to reinforce pupils' ability to identify their own 'trigger' situations

- to offer pupils the opportunity to discuss when there are 'trigger' situations that are common to many people

- to identify/recognise the physical reactions to strong feelings

- to introduce the significant trigger situation of bullying and provide pupils with the opportunity to share practical coping strategies for such situations

- to reinforce pupils' ability to reflect upon trigger situations and try to use the traffic light strategy for recognising, analysing and implementing a stepped approach to controlling strong feelings.

Group session – 45 minutes to 1 hour

Circle Warm-up – Angry dance

Before the session the facilitator will need to prepare a tape of various pieces of music. Each segment of music only needs to be about 30 seconds in length. This is most effective when at least some of the music segments are relevant to the pupils participating in the programme and varied in their beat and style, for example:

- Rap

- R&B

- Classical

- Pop

- Rock.

Within the circle, pupils are then encouraged to move to the music, making their movements reflect the way that the music makes them feel.

Activity One – My strong feelings diary review

At the close of the previous session the strong feelings diary was provided for the pupils. They were asked to complete it over the course of the week and to record any outbursts of anger in terms of:

- Triggers – what made them angry, upset or stressed?

- Feelings – when they became angry, upset or stressed what feelings/reactions did they notice within themselves?

- Behaviour – what they did when they experienced an escalation of strong feelings.

- Consequences – what happened next?

They were also asked to scale themselves on how well they coped with the escalation in strong feelings as marks out of 10.

0	5	10
Not well	OK	Brilliant

Within the Circle Time structure the facilitator now reviews the pupils' completed feelings diaries. Pupils are encouraged to share their successes and emotional triggers using the strong feelings diary review sheet. During this time it may be useful for pupils to discuss:

- triggers that caused them to become angry, upset or stressed

- what it felt like to be out of control

- what they did when they experienced an escalation of strong feelings

- what happened after they became angry, upset or out of control

- any successful calming strategies they used to de-escalate their strong feelings

Activity Two – Emotional story

Within the circle, the facilitator reads the emotional story to the group. This story details how two older pupils are bullying Mickey by ripping up his schoolbook, taking his money and now threatening to beat him up if he does not give them his mobile phone. When a girl witnesses and challenges their bullying, the bullies turn on her, slapping her face. This results in Mickey losing his temper, grabbing one of the bullies by the throat, pushing him to the floor and repeatedly kicking him in the head.

Activity Three – Question sheet

Pupils are then encouraged to analyse Mickey's behaviour and the possible feelings and emotions that may have triggered his outbursts. Thay are asked a series of ten questions that are aimed at identifying what strategies could have been used by Mickey to de-escalate his strong feelings. These are as follows:

1. Why didn't Mickey want to go to school?

2. What had Sid and Arun done to Mickey this last week?

3. What do you think of their behaviour?

4. Why did Mickey feel ashamed?

5. Why did Mickey look embarrassed when he saw Gemma?

6. Was Gemma brave to confront the bullies?

7. What caused Mickey to lose his temper?

8. What do you think 'should' happen next?

9. How would you cope in Mickey's situation?

10. How do people get help if they are being bullied in your school?

The pupil's responses can be recorded in note form by the facilitator using a whiteboard. This will take any stress out of the recording process and allow a focus on thinking as opposed to worrying about recording responses on paper. It may be helpful to enlarge the question sheet to A3 size to act as a prompt and visual reminder.

Activity Four – What makes me lose it?

In this activity the facilitator encourages pupils to reflect upon the situations that make them lose control. The pupils are asked to examine a series of statements describing what causes some people to lose control. Pupils are then encouraged to add to the list their own additional situations that may trigger their own strong feelings. This activity presents the pupils with an opportunity to use their reflective skills to analyse what situations trigger their anger, thus facilitating their ability to extract themselves from a situation before their feelings escalate. The facilitator may need to model the identification of triggers to the pupils. Although this activity is best completed on an individual basis, the facilitator can, if necessary, act as scribe for the group, with the majority of the task being conducted verbally within a circle discussion.

Once pupils have ticked the statements that apply to them, they can then note down up to three additional situations that trigger a loss of control. Upon completion of this activity the facilitator can encourage pupils to share their trigger situations and analyse any similarities or differences in responses.

Activity Five – Bully box

This activity is aimed at encouraging pupils to analyse how they could prevent bullying both in and out of the school context. Pupils are also asked to reflect upon how they could cope effectively when they encounter situations of bullying. Pupils can record their thoughts, ideas and strategies on the format provided. All answers could then be drawn together during a Circle Time feedback session. Alternatively, ideas can be fed back verbally if the majority of pupils have difficulties with the recording process.

The issue of bullying can be a central element to pupils experiencing difficulties in managing their strong feelings and behaviour. It is therefore important that the facilitator encourages pupils to genuinely reflect upon their own experiences of bullying. The stop, think and reflect section of the sheet format provided gives the facilitator a number of questions from which to initiate the group discussion;

- Have you ever felt like bullying someone?

- Why?

- What happened?

- What might you do differently next time if you felt this way?

7

This activity encourages pupils to consider the use of different types of physical exercise as a tool for 'working off' their strong feelings. On the format provided, pupils can record different physical ways in which they could reduce or re-channel their strong and uncomfortable emotions. The use of pictures (even stick people) may provide a more interesting way for pupils to record their ideas. The facilitator may have to model some suggestions for physical exercise that pupils could utilise. These might include the following;

- running
- jumping
- hopping
- skipping
- clapping
- clicking fingers
- kicking balls
- batting balls.

Within the circle, the facilitator can then draw all the suggestions together and offer the pupils an opportunity to share their ideas. Although this is an individualised activity the facilitator can, if necessary, act as scribe for the group, with the majority of the task being conducted verbally within a Circle Time discussion.

Plenary

The facilitator can prompt the pupils to review the session. It may be useful to focus on the following questions:

- What did you learn this session?
- How do you feel about this session?
- How do you think this session might help you in the future?
- What advice would you give us if we ran this session again?

At the close of the session pupils are given another page of the strong feelings diary in the format provided, which they will be asked to complete over the course of the coming week.

This diary can then be reviewed in the next session within a Circle Time discussion.

Strong Feelings Diary Review: Week 6

Name:..

Date: ....

Last week my strong feeling was:

The feeling was:

Good · Neutral · Bad

The trigger was:

My target for this week is:

I will watch out for these triggers:

*

*

*

I will try to cope with my strong feelings by thinking the following thoughts:

*

*

*

I will use the following strategies if I feel the EXPLOSION coming:

Signed: .... Date: ....

BULLY BOYS

Mickey didn't want to go to school. He felt really frightened because he knew that Sid and Arun would be waiting for him. They had waited every day that week. The first day they had taken his packed lunch. The second day they had ripped up his reading book which meant that he was now going to have to pay for it out of his pocket money. There was no way that he could have told Mr Hallford as it would just have made it worse. He had to pretend that his little baby brother had got hold of it and ripped out the pages. On Wednesday and Thursday they had stolen his money and Arun said that he wanted him to bring in his mobile phone on Friday so that they could sell it on and make some 'real' money out of him.

Mickey wished that he could tell someone. He felt ashamed and angry that they had been picking on him. It just wasn't fair. He hadn't done anything to them. Maybe they were doing it because he was the smallest boy in the class. He didn't know and he wouldn't dream of asking them.

Today was Friday and he just wished that it was over. He couldn't face it all again. As his mum dropped him off at the school gates he seriously considered making a run for it but he was stopped by his friend Gemma.

'Where are you going?' she asked. 'You're not thinking of bunking off are you?'

Mickey turned around and looked embarrassed. He was just about to tell her about the bullying when the bullies themselves suddenly approached them. Sid smirked at Mickey and said, 'It's little short arse – the ugly midget boy – let's hope he's got us a present.' 'Yeah – otherwise he's in for a right hammering', said Arun. Gemma looked astonished.

'Don't be such bullies,' she said. 'You can't talk to him like that. It's not right.'

Arun looked at her and laughed out loud. Then he slapped her hard across the face. 'Shut up!' he shouted. Mickey just lost it. He didn't even have time to think. He grabbed Arun by the throat, pulled him down to the ground and kicked his head again and again. He didn't hear the others shouting at him to stop. All he could hear was his own heart racing and all he could see was a haze of red heat in front of him.

Question Sheet

1. Why didn't Mickey want to go to school?

2. What had Sid and Arun done to Mickey this last week?

3. What do you think of their behaviour?

4. Why did Mickey feel ashamed?

5. Why did Mickey look embarrassed when he saw Gemma?

6. Was Gemma brave to confront the bullies?

7. What caused Mickey to lose his temper?

8. What do you think 'should' happen next?

9. How would you cope in Mickey's situation?

10. How do people get help if they are being bullied in your school?

What Makes Me Lose It?
Stop the match being lit!

Here is a list of statements describing what makes some people lose control. Tick the ones that are true for you and add some of your own that have not been listed.

- When people talk about me behind my back ....
- When I get my work wrong ....
- When other people get hurt ....
- When others won't play with me ....
- When I'm treated unfairly ....
- When I'm shouted at ....
- When people interfere with my games ....
- When people stop me doing what I want to ....
- When others get more attention than me ....
- When people call me names ....
- When I'm losing at football ....
- When people are rude about my family ....
- When people bully my friends ....
- When someone calls me a liar ....
- When someone pushes me or happy slaps me ....
- When I get told off and others don't ....
- When things get broken ....
- When someone takes my things ....
- When there is a lot of noise and I'm trying to concentrate ....
- When I have to do something I don't want to do ....
- When I'm told off in front of my friends ....
- When I get interrupted ....
- When people don't give me a chance ....
- When other people are angry ....
- When people don't listen to me ....
- When people don't understand me ....

Other things that make me lose control are:

- ....
- ....
- ....

Stop, think and discuss

- What do we have in common? What things make all of us lose control?

Bully Box

Everyone feels angry, hurt, upset and confused when they are bullied by others. What can we do in and out of school in order to prevent or cope better with bullying? Work together in order to complete this thoughtstorm.

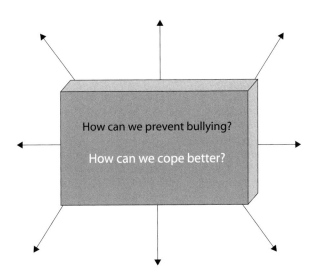

How can we prevent bullying?

How can we cope better?

Stop, think and reflect. Discuss in the group

- Have you ever felt like bullying someone? Why? What happened? What might you do differently next time if you felt this way?

Anger Strategy Sheet

Jump out your jealousy!

Move it

Run out your anger!

How can you shake off your uncomfortable feelings?

Record your ideas inside the balls.

Share your ideas with a friend. Does the use of physical exercise work for both of you?

What are the differences?

My Strong Feelings Diary: Week 7

This coming week think about one strong feeling that you have had. Draw a picture of what gave you this strong feeling (trigger); circle the feeling you had (feeling); what you did (behaviour) and what happened next (consequences).

Then scale yourself on a scale of 1 – 10 for how well you coped with your strong feeling.

0	1	2	3	4	5	6	7	8	9	10

Not Well   OK   Brilliant

What made you have this strong feeling (trigger)?

What strong feeling did you have?

Was this feeling

Good

Neutral

Bad

What did you do (behaviour)?

What happened next (consequences)?

How well did you cope with your strong feeling?

/10

How could you have coped better with this strong feeling?

Controlling Anger

Session 8
Listen-up!

Resources to photocopy or print from the CD-ROM

Strong Feelings Diary Review: Week 7

Listen-up! emotional story

Question Sheet

Behaviour Thoughtstorms

Strong Feelings Log

Getting to Zero

My Strong Feelings Diary: Week 8

Session 8: Listen-up!

Aims of the session

- to focus on identifying solutions and alternatives to negative reactions
- to encourage pupils to be reflective about how their behaviour triggers the strong feelings in others
- to identify self-management strategies and methods which may impact positively on behaviours
- to introduce the principle of the tension scale to de-escalate uncomfortable feelings
- to reinforce pupils' ability to reflect upon trigger situations and utilise a strategy to assist them in recognising, analysing and implementing a stepped approach to controlling strong feelings.

Group session – 45 minutes to 1 hour

Circle Warm-up – Pass the face

Pupils need to be seated in a circle for this activity. The facilitator demonstrates an emotion on her own face. The facilitator then turns to the pupil sitting next to her and the pupil then 'assumes' the face. Once the face has been 'passed' to each person in the circle, another person takes a turn to create a face, which is then passed around each person in the circle. If pupils find the expression difficult to copy the facilitator may have to prompt them. The following emotions may be useful to work from if needed:

- happiness
- surprise
- excitement
- shock
- anger
- annoyance.

Activity One – My strong feelings diary review

At the close of the previous session the strong feelings diary was handed out to pupils. They were asked to complete it over the course of the week and to record any outbursts of anger in terms of:

- Triggers – what made them angry, upset or stressed?
- Feelings – when they became angry, upset or stressed what feelings/reactions did they notice within themselves?
- Behaviour – what they did when they experienced an escalation of strong feelings.
- Consequences – what happened next?

They were also asked to scale themselves on how well they coped with the escalation in strong feelings as marks out of 10.

0	5	10
Not well	OK	Brilliant

Within the Circle Time structure the facilitator now reviews the pupils' completed feelings diaries. Pupils are encouraged to share their successes and emotional triggers using the strong feelings diary review sheet. During this time it may be useful for pupils to discuss:

- triggers that caused them to become angry, upset or stressed
- what it felt like to be out of control
- what they did when they experienced an escalation of strong feelings
- what happened after they became angry, upset or out of control
- any successful calming strategies they used to de-escalate their strong feelings.

Activity Two – Emotional story

The facilitator reads the emotional story to the group. This story details how Frankie is set a specific maths problem solving exercise with two of his peers. After struggling to understand what is expected of them, Frankie approaches the teacher to seek advice and help. Instead of listening to the pupils' difficulties and providing the expected assistance, Mr Lucas refuses to help the pupils and demands they solve the problem themselves. Following the teacher's refusal to listen or even discuss his group's difficulty, Frankie becomes so furious that he pushes the teacher's desk and accuses him of not being a proper teacher.

Activity Three – Question sheet

Pupils are then encouraged to analyse Frankie's behaviour and the possible feelings and emotions that may have triggered his outbursts. The facilitator asks pupils a series of ten questions. These are as follows:

1. Why did Frankie like his school?
2. Why did Frankie breathe a sigh of relief?
3. What was the problem solving task set by Mr Lucas?
4. Why did Mr Lucas tell the group to just 'get on with it'?
5. Was he right to do this?
6. How would you have felt if you were in Frankie's shoes?
7. Was Frankie right to say that Mr Lucas wasn't a 'proper' teacher?
8. How could Frankie have coped better in this situation?

9. What would you have done in Frankie's position? How would you have coped with your anger and frustration?

10. What do you think will happen next?

The pupils' responses can be recorded in note form by the facilitator using a whiteboard. This will take any stress out of the recording process and allow for a focus on thinking as opposed to worrying about recording responses on paper. It may be helpful to enlarge the question sheet to A3 size for this purpose.

Activity Four – Behaviour thoughtstorms

In this activity the facilitator encourages pupils to reflect upon the behaviours that do and do not generate anger and stress. In pairs or even as a group, they can work through the format provided and record anger generating or preventing behaviours from their own experience. The facilitator can, if necessary, act as scribe for the group, with the majority of the task being conducted verbally within the circle.

Activity Five – Strong feelings log

This activity is aimed at encouraging pupils to consider and analyse how they manage their behaviour over the course of the coming week in all settings: home, school and elsewhere. The facilitator should give the sheet to the pupils and explain that they need to choose somebody (themselves, their parent/carer or teacher) to complete it over the coming week. Pupils need to understand that the strong feelings log is aimed at assessing their progress so far.

Activity Six – Getting to zero

This activity encourages pupils to identify how tense they are feeling on a tension scale ranging from zero (calm and relaxed) to ten (extremely tense). By using the stepped approach (in the format provided), they can become more reflective about situations that cause them to feel tense and angry. They then hopefully become more able to identify the root of their difficulty and thus select an appropriate method by which they can tackle and resolve their problem.

The facilitator may wish to model the use of the tension scale strategy to the group. Using the following example situations may be a helpful starting point:

I am angry and stressed because:

- somebody did not do what they said they were going to do
- someone said something about my family
- I was called a name
- I was tackled badly during a game of football.

I am on point 9 of the scale

In order to get down to point 2 I need to...

- count to ten
- have some time out

- talk to someone about how I am feeling
- participate in some physical exercise
- visualise a calm place in my mind
- say to myself, 'It doesn't matter, it is not life or death'.

When I am on zero I will feel...
- calm
- happy
- relaxed
- less tense
- safe
- secure.

Plenary

The facilitator can prompt the pupils to review the session. It may be useful to focus on the following questions;
- What did you learn this session?
- How do you feel about this session?
- How do you think this session might help you in the future?
- What advice would you give us if we ran this session again?

At the close of the session pupils are given another page of the strong feelings diary in the format provided, which they will be asked to complete over the course of the coming week.

This diary can then be reviewed in the next session within a Circle Time discussion.

Strong Feelings Diary Review: Week 7

Name: ....

Date: ....

Last week my strong feeling was:

The feeling was:

Good	Neutral	Bad

The trigger was:

My target for this week is:

I will watch out for these triggers:

-
-
-

I will try to cope with my strong feelings by thinking the following thoughts:

-
-
-

I will use the following strategies if I feel the EXPLOSION coming:

Signed: .... Date: ....

LISTEN-UP!

Frankie was looking forward to meeting his new teacher. He had always loved his school, not because of the work they did particularly, but mainly because he enjoyed being with his friends. He loved having a laugh and playing football and was looking forward to being in the school team this term. He didn't find the work that easy but Mrs Mitchell was there to help him and had stayed with him since Year 2. It was the first day of the Autumn term and Frankie felt happy.

When the bell rang for registration Frankie followed the rest of his class into Room 7 where Mr Lucas was waiting. He looked OK as he smiled when the children came into the room. Frankie breathed a sigh of relief. He hadn't really wanted to admit it but he had felt a bit nervous about meeting Mr Lucas for the first time. Mr Lucas took the register and then told the class what they had to do in the Maths session. It was a problem solving task and Frankie was asked to work in a group with Caris and Amy. They had to build a bridge out of card but to very specific measurements.

'This looks OK,' said Frankie.

He called out Mr Lucas's name and waited for him to approach the table.

'Yes – what is it?' he asked.

'We're not quite sure how to measure this bit sir,' said Frankie.

Mr Lucas looked a little red in the face.

'That's the whole point – it's a problem solving exercise,' he said. 'You've got to work it out together – so just get on with it.' He then walked away and sat at his desk taking out a sports magazine from the top drawer. Frankie looked at the two girls. He felt slightly embarrassed but also a little bit angry that Mr Lucas hadn't helped them. 'I suppose we'd better have another go.' he said.

Unfortunately, Mrs Mitchell was away, as her own daughter was ill that day, so there was no one else to ask. The group continued to try and work out the problem for another 10 minutes by which time Amy was beginning to look tearful.

'I'll ask Sir again,' said Frankie and he walked over to the teacher's desk.

'Sir, we really need help,' he said. Mr Lucas looked up. 'Yes – and you can help each other,' he said frostily. 'B...b...ut... we need help from you – you need to listen to us,' said Frankie.

'No – I need you just to go back to your seat and do the work I've set for you,' said Mr Lucas.

Frankie was furious. He pushed the teacher's desk and thumped his fist on top of the pile of books. 'Why can't you listen?' he screamed. 'You're not a proper teacher. A proper teacher would listen and help and show us how to do stuff. You're just a big fat bully!' He kicked the desk and then ran out of the room. Mr Lucas stared after him. He looked totally shocked.

Question Sheet

1. Why did Frankie like his school?

2. Why did Frankie breathe a sigh of relief?

3. What was the problem solving task set by Mr Lucas?

4. Why did Mr Lucas tell the group to just 'get on with it'?

5. Was he right to do this?

6. How would you have felt if you were in Frankie's shoes?

7. Was Frankie right to say that Mr Lucas wasn't a 'proper' teacher?

8. How could Frankie have coped better in this situation?

9. What would you have done in Frankie's position? How would you have coped with your anger and frustration?

10. What do you think will happen next?

Behaviour Thoughtstorms

What do we do that may make others feel angry or stressed? What can we do to ensure that we don't make people feel this way? Work together and complete the two thoughtstorms below. Can you agree?

Behaviours that generate anger and stress

Behaviours that don't generate anger and stress

Strong Feelings Log Check-up Time!

Keep this log for one week in order to check-up on your skills. How are you doing? Have you developed your strategies?

This may be completed by a) you b) your teacher or c) your parent/carer – you choose!

Name:.. School:..

Circle the number that best describes your feelings.

Self- Management

Strong Feelings at School	Poor		Good		Excellent
Monday	1	2	3	4	5
Tuesday	1	2	3	4	5
Wednesday	1	2	3	4	5
Thursday	1	2	3	4	5
Friday	1	2	3	4	5

Strong Feelings at Home					
Monday	1	2	3	4	5
Tuesday	1	2	3	4	5
Wednesday	1	2	3	4	5
Thursday	1	2	3	4	5
Friday	1	2	3	4	5
Saturday	1	2	3	4	5
Sunday	1	2	3	4	5

Strong Feelings Elsewhere (trips etc)					
Monday	1	2	3	4	5
Tuesday	1	2	3	4	5
Wednesday	1	2	3	4	5
Thursday	1	2	3	4	5
Friday	1	2	3	4	5
Saturday	1	2	3	4	5
Sunday	1	2	3	4	5

Completed by:.. (Child/Teacher/Parent/Carer)

Getting to Zero

Use the tension scale to sort out your problem!

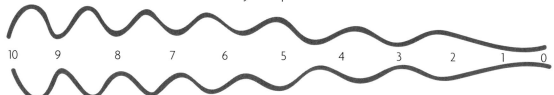

10   9   8   7   6   5   4   3   2   1   0

Complete the steps:

1. I am upset because...

....

....

2. I am on point .... on the scale.

3. To get down to point .... I need to ...

....

....

4. To get down to point zero I need to...

....

....

5. When I am on zero I will feel...

....

....

My Strong Feelings Diary: Week 8

This coming week think about one strong feeling that you have had. Draw a picture of what gave you this strong feeling (trigger); circle the feeling you had (feeling); what you did (behaviour) and what happened next (consequences).

Then scale yourself on a scale of 1 – 10 for how well you coped with your strong feeling.

Not Well	OK	Brilliant

What made you have this strong feeling (trigger)?

What strong feeling did you have?

Was this feeling

Good

Neutral

Bad

What did you do (behaviour)?

What happened next (consequences)?

How well did you cope with your strong feeling?

/10

How could you have coped better with this strong feeling?

Controlling Anger

Session 9
All Alone

Resources to photocopy or print from the CD-ROM

Strong Feelings Diary Review: Week 8

All Alone emotional story

Question Sheet

Strategy Information Sheet

Dampen the Fuse

The Script

Personal Strategy Sheet

Relaxation Tip Sheet

My Strong Feelings Diary: Week 9

Session 9: All Alone

Aims of the session

- to focus on identifying solutions and alternatives to negative reactions
- to identify anger and stress management strategies and methods which may have a positive impact
- to recognise that feeling stressed can lead to negative outcomes and behaviours
- to reinforce the pupils' ability to implement different self-help strategies
- to reinforce the strategy of 'relaxing' to enable pupils to wind down from strong and uncomfortable feelings
- to reinforce pupils' ability to reflect upon trigger situations and the need to stop, think, reflect and discuss their emotions in order to gain control and find positive solutions.

Group session – 45 minutes to 1 hour

Circle Warm-up – Memory game

Within the circle pupils play a memory game. They are asked to recall all the reasons that Ashley becomes distressed. The facilitator begins the session by stating that Ashley got distressed on Monday because his mum yelled at him. The next pupil in the circle then states the previous reason that Ashley became upset and adds one of their own. This continues until everyone in the group has had a turn. Some of the following ideas may be useful to get the game going:

Ashley got upset on Monday because...

- he got pushed in the line outside his class
- he got fouled in football
- someone took his favourite pencil case
- someone said something horrible about his family
- his teacher would not listen to him
- a boy swore at him
- someone looked at him the 'wrong way'
- his drink squashed his sandwiches.

Activity One – My strong feelings diary review

At the close of the previous session the strong feelings diary was handed out to pupils. They were asked to complete it over the course of the week and to record any outbursts of anger in terms of:

- Triggers – what made them angry, upset or stressed?

- Feelings – when they became angry, upset or stressed what feelings/reactions did they notice within themselves?

- Behaviour – what they did when they experienced an escalation of strong feelings.

- Consequences – what happened next?

They were also asked to scale themselves on how well they coped with the escalation in strong feelings as marks out of 10.

| 0 | 5 | 10 |
| Not well | OK | Brilliant |

Within the Circle Time structure the facilitator now reviews the pupils' completed feelings diaries. Pupils are encouraged to share their successes and emotional triggers using the strong feelings diary review sheet. During this time it may be useful for pupils to discuss:

- triggers that caused them to become angry, upset or stressed

- what it felt like to be out of control

- what they did when they experienced an escalation of strong feelings

- what happened after they became angry, upset or out of control

- any successful calming strategies they used to de-escalate their strong feelings.

Activity Two – Emotional story

Within the circle, the facilitator reads the emotional story to the group. This story describes how a young boy called Marcus moves from a London city school to a small village school on the South coast. Having left all of his friends behind in London he feels very isolated and lonely. He feels so isolated from his peers that he decides not to talk to anyone or even show any emotions. The teachers at the school become worried and they contact Marcus's mother to explain what is happening. She consequently has a go at him, accusing him of being an awkward 'brat'. Marcus's feelings of isolation continue to grow and while watching the other pupils play football his anger explodes and he begins a fight with the boy who scores a goal.

Activity Three – Question sheet

Pupils are then encouraged to analyse Marcus's behaviour and the possible feelings and emotions that may have triggered his outbursts. They are asked a series of ten questions which are aimed at getting them to suggest what strategies could have been used by Marcus to de-escalate the situation. These are as follows:

1. Why did Marcus hate his new school?

2. Where had Marcus moved from and how do you think this place was different to his new home?

3. Was Marcus right to refuse to speak to anyone?

4. Why did he feel jealous of the other children?

5. What advice would you have given to him?

6. Why did things 'explode' on the Friday afternoon?

7. Why do you think Marcus picked on Jonathan?

8. How could he have coped better with his angry feelings?

9. How do you think his mum will feel about his behaviour?

10. What do you think will happen next?

The children's responses can be recorded in note form by the facilitator using a whiteboard. This will take any stress out of the recording process and allow for a focus on thinking as opposed to worrying about recording responses on paper. It may be helpful to enlarge the question sheet to A3 size.

Activity Four – Strategy information sheet

Here the facilitator encourages pupils to reflect upon all of the different stress and anger management strategies examined over the course of the programme. Within the circle, the facilitator can encourage pupils to examine the variety of strategies and analyse which ones are most effective for them and why. Basically this is a, 'What works for you?' session. The facilitator may need to model how the strategies have been used by the pupils. The format provides details the different strategies as follows:

Self-talk Sort a personal script to self-calm.	Check thinking Untwist your thoughts from negatives to positives.	Talk it through Describe the behaviour and de-personalise it.
Use 'I' statements They don't blame others and allow you to be open and honest.	Joint approach Ask a friend to help/ support you.	Broken record technique Devise a mini repetitive script to calm down.
Use humour Deflect yourself and think funny.	Consider choices What can you 'choose' to do differently?	Time out Make sure it's the 'right' place and amount of time– plan ahead.

On the sheet provided pupils can then note down up to three additional strategies that they have found successful in the management of their own stress and anger.

Activity Five – Dampen the fuse

This activity is aimed at encouraging pupils to consider the effects of stress. The facilitator can initiate a group discussion that encourages pupils to identify their triggers to stress. The following prompts may help to get the discussion going:

I feel stressed when…

- I cannot understand what the teacher wants me to do
- other people are finishing their work quicker than me
- the drawings done by others look better than mine
- we are losing at football
- I forget my homework and the teacher has a go at me.

Pupils can then identify strategies they can use to reduce such feelings. The effects of implementing a practical strategy to 'relax' can then be analysed. Pupils can be given an opportunity to identify how 'relaxing' could impact positively on their feelings and behaviours. They can record their thoughts, ideas and strategies on the format provided. All answers could then be drawn together during a Circle Time feedback discussion.

Activity Six – The script

This activity encourages pupils to develop a personal script to enable them to stop, wait, reflect and go. This stepped script approach is as follows:

Stop

- What are you feeling?
- Identify your early warning signs.
- Check your thinking.
- Check your 'state' – breathe deeply and less quickly.

Wait

- What is your point of reference? – Remember routines/directions.
- Identify useful strategies that can be used in the situation.

Reflect

- Respond rather than react.
- Check tone and pitch of voice.
- Check gestures and diffuse instinctive reactions.
- Check proximity.
- Keep eye contact.

Go

- Put into action rehearsed words/phrases/statements/techniques that can be used.

By reflecting upon all the above areas, pupils identify and then note down a personal script that they can work through in order to effectively relax themselves. They can record their scripts on the format provided. Pupils who have difficulties in recording can be allocated a scribe (either the facilitator or a peer). Within the circle the facilitator can then draw all the suggestions together and offer the pupils an opportunity to share their ideas.

Activity Seven – Personal strategy sheet

This activity encourages pupils to identify ways in which they can 'wind down' when they feel stressed within or by a situation. On the format provided, they can draw the different ways in which they 'chill-out'.

The facilitator can then draw all the suggestions together and offer the pupils an opportunity to share their ideas.

Activity Eight – Relaxation

Before the pupils leave, the facilitator can talk them through this tip sheet, reminding them that they can employ this strategy to effectively reduce their stress levels. The facilitator will need to give each of the pupils a copy of the tip sheet to take home. This will enable both class teacher and parents to support the pupils in practising this strategy.

Plenary

The facilitator can prompt the pupils to review the session. It may be useful to focus on the following questions;

- What did you learn this session?
- How do you feel about this session?
- How do you think this session might help you in the future?
- What advice would you give us if we ran this session again?

At the close of the session pupils are given another page of the strong feelings diary on the format provided, which they will be asked to complete over the course of the coming week.

This diary can then be reviewed in the next session within a Circle Time discussion.

9

Strong Feelings Diary Review: Week 8

Name:...

Date: ....

Last week my strong feeling was:

The feeling was:

Good   Neutral   Bad

The trigger was:

My target for this week is:

I will watch out for these triggers:

•

•

•

I will try to cope with my strong feelings by thinking the following thoughts:

•

•

•

I will use the following strategies if I feel the EXPLOSION coming:

Signed: .... Date: ....

ALL ALONE

Marcus hated his new school. He was the only black boy in his class and he felt totally alone from the start. He had moved from London to a small village on the South coast when his mum and dad had divorced last year. Right from the start he knew that he wouldn't fit in. All the other kids had known each other right through school. They went to the same clubs and had the same hobbies – mainly horse riding. Marcus hadn't even seen a horse (let alone got on one and ridden it) before they moved out of London. He knew he would never fit in with them. He just didn't share their interests and never would. He felt as if he was some sort of freak.

Every day at school, he would sit on his own at the back of the class. He did the work and concentrated but he didn't smile or say one word to anyone else in the class if he could help it. He tried to look as if he didn't care but inside he felt angry, sad and very alone.

After he'd been at Chalfont Primary for about six weeks he made up his mind that he would simply stop talking to anyone at all – even the teachers. After about a week of this, it was clear that Miss Hurst was getting worried about him. She continually asked if he was OK. She looked really upset when he refused to answer. He simply nodded his head.

Playtimes were the worst. He simply stood by the side of the football pitch and watched the others play. Deep down, he would have loved to play too but he knew that he would need to talk to the others to do that. The real problem was that he was now beginning to feel really angry inside and jealous of all the other kids in his class who seemed to be so happy and have so many friends to go about with. He was especially angry with the most popular boys in his class – watching them playing football made him furious. He just felt so left out.

Then, one Friday afternoon, things just seemed to explode. He'd had a bad morning as his mum had got a letter from the school telling her that he was acting mute. They wanted him to see some sort of psychologist. His mum was furious. 'You're just being an awkward brat,' she said. That afternoon the boys were playing a really good match. Marcus had watched from the side, getting more and more angry as he saw how much fun they were having. Suddenly he just exploded. He didn't stop to think. He ran out onto the pitch and began to kick Jonathan who had just scored a goal. Jonathan hit back and in no time the two boys were fighting in the centre of the pitch while the rest of the class looked on in utter amazement and shock.

Question Sheet

1. Why did Marcus hate his new school?

2. Where had Marcus moved from and how do you think this place was different to his new home?

3. Was Marcus right to refuse to speak to anyone?

4. Why did he feel jealous of the other children?

5. What advice would you have given to him?

6. Why did things 'explode' on the Friday afternoon?

7. Why do you think Marcus picked on Jonathan?

8. How could he have coped better with his angry feelings?

9. How do you think his mum will feel about his behaviour?

10. What do you think will happen next?

Strategy Information Sheet
Stress and Anger Management

Which strategies could you use? Stop, think, reflect and discuss.

Self-talk Sort a personal script to self-calm.	**Check thinking** Untwist your thoughts from negatives to positives.	**Talk it through** Describe the behaviour and de-personalise it.
Use 'I' statements They don't blame others and allow you to be open and honest.	**Joint approach** Ask a friend to help/ support you.	**Broken record technique** Devise a mini repetitive script to calm down.
Use humour Deflect yourself and think funny.	**Consider choices** What can you 'choose' to do differently?	**Time out** Make sure it's the 'right' place and amount of time— plan ahead.
Personal strategy	Personal strategy	Personal strategy

9

Dampen the Fuse

Sometimes we feel stressed and this then leads on to negative behaviours. We need to recognise personal triggers to STRESS and to try to dampen the fuse by using positive strategies. STOP, THINK AND REFLECT – identify your triggers to stress and strategies you can use to prevent stress turning into angry feelings!

Use the format below to record your ideas...

Trigger to stress	What can I do? What STRATEGY?	How will I feel and behave if I use my strategy?
1.		
2.		
3.		
4.		
5.		

Discuss with a friend – how are your stressors and strategies the same and how are they different?

The Script

Stop!   What am I feeling? (Check your early warning signs.)

             What is happening here? (Check your thinking.)

             Check your 'state' (Breathe deeply and less quickly.)

Wait!   What is my point of reference? (Remember rules/routines/directions.)

             What strategies can I use for this situation? (Recall your contingency plan.)

Reflect!   Respond rather that react.

             • Check your tone of voice and its pitch

             • Check your gestures and diffuse instinctive reactions

             • Check your proximity

             • Keep eye contact

GO!   What rehearsed words/phrases/statements/techniques shall I use?

Write your script here.

Personal Strategy Sheet
Wind Down

Everyone needs to relax. Relaxing and having a 'quiet' time can help us to cope with angry feelings. Draw and label the ways that you chill-out.

Relaxation Tip Sheet

- Choose a quiet room and a time when you're unlikely to be disturbed.

- Wear very light clothing.

- Lie on your back on the floor or a firm surface.

- Tense the muscles in your right foot and ankle. Wriggle your toes.
  How does it feel? Clench the muscles and release them several times.
  Notice the difference in sensation between the clenched and
  unclenched muscles. Commit it to memory.

- Repeat the exercise with your left foot and ankle.

- Tense the calf muscles, first one then the other.
  Repeat several times, alternately clenching and unclenching.
  Once again notice the difference in sensation between the tense and
  the relaxed state. Remember it.

- Move next to the thigh muscles and carry out the same exercise.
  Notice how tension in the thighs affects the kneecaps and the knees.

- Now move to the muscles of the bottom.
  Notice once more the difference in sensation between tension and relaxation.

- Work upwards, taking in the muscles of the abdomen, of the chest and
  of the back and shoulders, working upon each group in turn.

- Now work on the biceps, the forearms and the hands.

- Lastly, move to the neck, the jaw, the face and forehead, and the scalp.

- Try this strategy.
- Ask your teacher to talk you through it.
- Can you use this at home? Discuss.

9

Session 9

My Strong Feelings Diary: Week 9

This coming week think about one strong feeling that you have had. Draw a picture of what gave you this strong feeling (trigger); circle the feeling you had (feeling); what you did (behaviour) and what happened next (consequences).

Then scale yourself on a scale of 1 – 10 for how well you coped with your strong feeling.

0	1	2	3	4	5	6	7	8	9	10

Not Well   OK   Brilliant

What made you have this strong feeling (trigger)?

What strong feeling did you have?

Was this feeling

Good

Neutral

Bad

What did you do (behaviour)?

What happened next (consequences)?

How well did you cope with your strong feeling?

/10

How could you have coped better with this strong feeling?

Controlling Anger

Session 10
Review and Evaluation

Resources to photocopy or print from the CD-ROM

Observation Checklist (Staff)

Thoughtstorm Activity

Course Evaluation

Top Targets

Completion Certificate

'Being Me' Rap

Session 10: Review and Evaluation

Aims of the session

- to reinforce pupils ability to stop, think, reflect and discuss their behaviour
- to provide pupils with the opportunity to evaluate the progress they have made with managing their strong feeling and behaviours
- to provide pupils with the opportunity to plan ahead in managing their behaviours and feelings.

Group session – 45 minutes to 1 hour

Circle Warm-up – Circle pairs

Pupils will need to be paired up with someone in the group who is not a close friend. Within the circle, the facilitator then gives the pupils a topic to discuss with their partner. Remaining within the circle, pupils then 'interview' their partner to establish their thoughts/ ideas/information on the given topic. Each time a new topic is given the pupils are given two minutes to find out what their partner thinks/knows. After the time is up, the facilitator moves around the circle encouraging each pupil to feed back to the group about what their partner thinks, e.g. 'This is Sam and he thinks…'. To ensure that the pupils remain focused, the facilitator will need to maintain the pace of the session by limiting the amount of time that they have to discuss each of the given topics. The time allocation may have to be increased depending upon the active involvement of the pupils.

Here are some topics that you may find useful to get the game going:

- favourite football team
- good things to do with your friends
- favourite sports
- favourite film stars
- favourite films/TV programmes.

The important thing to remember during this game is to offer a lot of positive praise to those pupils who work well together and keep focused.

Activity One – My strong feelings diary review

At the close of the previous session the strong feelings diary was handed out to pupils. They were asked to complete it over the course of the week and to record any outbursts of anger in terms of:

- Triggers – what made them angry, upset or stressed?
- Feelings – when they became angry, upset or stressed what feelings/reactions did they notice within themselves?

- Behaviour – what they did when they experienced an escalation of strong feelings.

- Consequences – what happened next?

They were also asked to scale themselves on how well they coped with the escalation in strong feelings as marks out of 10.

0	5	10
Not well	OK	Brilliant

Within the Circle Time structure the facilitator now reviews the pupils' feelings diaries completed during the course. Pupils are encouraged to share their successes and emotional triggers.

During this time it may be useful for pupils to discuss:

- triggers that caused them to become angry, upset or stressed

- what it felt like to be out of control

- what they did when they experienced an escalation of strong feelings

- what happened after they became angry, upset or out of control

- any successful calming strategies they used to de-escalate their strong feelings.

Activity Two – Thoughtstorm activity

This is a thoughtstorming exercise that provides pupils with the opportunity to list and recall what they have learnt about their strong feelings. We recommend that the facilitator acts as scribe for the group and notes down the suggestions of the pupils. If needed, the facilitator may prompt pupils to recall important information. The following prompts may be useful:

- physical reactions

- heart beats faster

- hands get hot

- mouth gets dry

- breathe more quickly

- I feel panicky.

In addition to recalling triggers to strong feelings, pupils are also encouraged to recall skills that can be used to control them. The following prompts may be useful:

- Take deep breaths.

- Think about a calming place.

- Walk away.

- Ask for some time out.

- Talk to a friend.

- Talk to a teacher.

Activity Three – Course evaluation

During this activity, pupils evaluate their own progress in terms of their knowledge and skills/development. On the evaluation sheet format provided, pupils rate themselves against each of the statements on a scale of 0 – 10 (0 = not very much/never; 5 = a medium amount/ sometimes; 10 = a lot/almost always). We recommend that the facilitator reads through each of the statements. This will help to alleviate any anxieties that the pupils may feel about their reading ability or understanding of the task. It may also be necessary for the facilitator to conduct the evaluation with each individual pupil. Although this is time consuming, we have found it to be the most beneficial stress-free way of conducting the evaluation. The statements on the form are as follows:

- I understand why I get angry.

- I understand why others get angry.

- I know my triggers and what lights my fuse.

- I know how to stop my fuse from being lit.

- I know what happens to my body when I get angry.

- I understand the Assault Cycle and how I am vulnerable as I calm down.

- I know that I can cope when other children get angry.

- I know that I can cope when adults get angry.

- I can reflect on my behaviours.

- I can set sensible targets for change.

- I can use traffic lights to problem solve.

- I can use self-calming strategies (e.g. counting, deep breathing, relaxation).

- I can use self-talk and create my own scripts.

- I can use time out effectively.

- I can use 'I' messages.

- I can problem solve with friends.

- I can problem solve with adults.

- I can manage my stress.

- I can understand how others are feeling and change my behaviours towards them if I think they are getting angry.

The final aspect of the course evaluation requires pupils to rate each of the six parts of the sessions:

1. Circle games.

2. Emotional stories.

3. Question sessions.

4. Activity sheets.

5. Strategy sheets.

6. Plenary sessions.

Activity Four – Top targets

The previous aspects of this session have allowed the pupils to reflect upon the progress they have made to date. Now the facilitator needs to encourage them to reflect upon what steps they need to take now in order to continue the development of their skills in the future. The format provided invites pupils to identify three different skills that need further development. They then establish under what circumstances they could use these skills. In order to ascertain if their use of each skill has been helpful, the pupils note success criteria. Taking into account the difficulties faced by each of the pupils, the facilitator may need to prompt them in the identification of appropriate skills, situations and success criteria.

Plenary

As this is the final session of the course the facilitator may wish to prepare a set of course certificates for each of the pupils who have participated. A certificate format has been provided. However, pupils tend to respond more enthusiastically to such an award if they appear to be individualised. To this end we recommend that you copy the certificates onto different-coloured paper or card. Stickers/glitter etc could be added if appropriate. Taking the certificate home to share with their family would also be a lovely bonus for the pupils.

Post Course Teacher Evaluation

Once the course has been completed by the pupils, the facilitator should complete the observation checklist provided. This enables staff to highlight specific concerns or difficulties that may have been reduced as a result of the course. This evaluation sheet also enables the facilitator to take an after measurement of the pupils' progress. Hopefully, the observation checklist will reflect a reduced score, indicating an improvement in the pupils' ability to manage their behaviours and strong feelings.

Observation Checklist

Post Course Assessment

Name:..

Please circle the number which your observations suggest is most appropriate now that the above student has completed the Controlling Anger course.

	Always	Usually	Some-times	Never	Comment
1. Comes to school/class happily	1	2	3	4	
2. Settles in class without fuss	1	2	3	4	
3. Settles in small groups easily	1	2	3	4	
4. Follows class routines	1	2	3	4	
5. Accepts teacher's directions	1	2	3	4	
6. Accepts other pupils taking the lead	1	2	3	4	
7. Appears popular with other children	1	2	3	4	
8. Has at least one good friend	1	2	3	4	
9. Plays appropriately with other children	1	2	3	4	
10. Copes well with disappointment	1	2	3	4	
11. Appears confident	1	2	3	4	
12. Feels good about themselves	1	2	3	4	
13. Concentrates well	1	2	3	4	
14. Controls anger when provoked	1	2	3	4	
15. Has insight into own behaviour	1	2	3	4	
16. Learns from mistakes	1	2	3	4	
17. Keeps hands, feet, objects to themselves	1	2	3	4	
18. Hurts self	4	3	2	1	
19. Distracts other children	4	3	2	1	
20. Hurts other children	4	3	2	1	
Total					

Best score = 20   Worst score = 80

Completed by:...Date: ....

Session 10

10

Thoughtstorm Activity

Work together. STOP, THINK, REFLECT and DISCUSS.

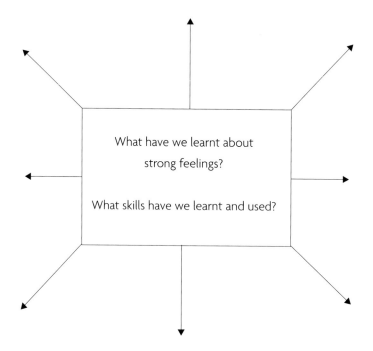

What have we learnt about
strong feelings?

What skills have we learnt and used?

Controlling Anger

Name: ....

School: ....

Date completed: ....

On the following pages rate yourself against each of the statements on a scale of 0 – 10

0 = not very much/never:

5 = a medium amount/sometimes:

10 = a lot/almost always.

Controlling Anger –
Course Evaluation: My Knowledge

How would you rate each aspect of the course? Use the scale 0 – 10 (0 = not good: 5 = sometimes OK: 10 = excellent)

I understand why I get angry.

| 0 | 1 | 2 | 3 | 4 | 5 | 6 | 7 | 8 | 9 | 10 |

I understand why others get angry.

| 0 | 1 | 2 | 3 | 4 | 5 | 6 | 7 | 8 | 9 | 10 |

I know my triggers and what lights my fuse.

| 0 | 1 | 2 | 3 | 4 | 5 | 6 | 7 | 8 | 9 | 10 |

I know how to stop my fuse from being lit.

| 0 | 1 | 2 | 3 | 4 | 5 | 6 | 7 | 8 | 9 | 10 |

I know what happens to my body when I get angry.

| 0 | 1 | 2 | 3 | 4 | 5 | 6 | 7 | 8 | 9 | 10 |

I understand the Assault Cycle and how I am vulnerable as I calm down.

| 0 | 1 | 2 | 3 | 4 | 5 | 6 | 7 | 8 | 9 | 10 |

I know that I can cope when other children get angry.

| 0 | 1 | 2 | 3 | 4 | 5 | 6 | 7 | 8 | 9 | 10 |

I know that I can cope when adults get angry.

| 0 | 1 | 2 | 3 | 4 | 5 | 6 | 7 | 8 | 9 | 10 |

Controlling Anger –
Course Evaluation: My Skills

I can reflect on my behaviours.

```
0      1      2      3      4      5      6      7      8      9      10
```

I can set realistic targets for change.

```
0      1      2      3      4      5      6      7      8      9      10
```

I can plan ahead and predict my behaviours.

```
0      1      2      3      4      5      6      7      8      9      10
```

I can use traffic lights to problem solve.

```
0      1      2      3      4      5      6      7      8      9      10
```

I can use self-calming strategies (e.g. counting, deep breathing, relaxation).

```
0      1      2      3      4      5      6      7      8      9      10
```

I can use self-talk and create my own scripts.

```
0      1      2      3      4      5      6      7      8      9      10
```

I can use time out effectively.

```
0      1      2      3      4      5      6      7      8      9      10
```

I can use 'I' messages.

```
0      1      2      3      4      5      6      7      8      9      10
```

I can problem solve with friends.

```
0      1      2      3      4      5      6      7      8      9      10
```

I can problem solve with adults.

```
0      1      2      3      4      5      6      7      8      9      10
```

I can manage my stress.

```
0      1      2      3      4      5      6      7      8      9      10
```

I can understand how others are feeling and change my behaviours towards them if I think they are getting angry.

```
0      1      2      3      4      5      6      7      8      9      10
```

Session 10

10

Controlling Anger –
Course Evaluation

How would you rate each aspect of the course? Use the scale 0 – 10 (0 = not good: 5 = sometimes OK: 10 = excellent)

1. Circle games

| 0 | 1 | 2 | 3 | 4 | 5 | 6 | 7 | 8 | 9 | 10 |

2. Emotional stories

| 0 | 1 | 2 | 3 | 4 | 5 | 6 | 7 | 8 | 9 | 10 |

3. Question sessions

| 0 | 1 | 2 | 3 | 4 | 5 | 6 | 7 | 8 | 9 | 10 |

4. Activity sheets

| 0 | 1 | 2 | 3 | 4 | 5 | 6 | 7 | 8 | 9 | 10 |

5. Strategy sheets

| 0 | 1 | 2 | 3 | 4 | 5 | 6 | 7 | 8 | 9 | 10 |

6. Plenary sessions

| 0 | 1 | 2 | 3 | 4 | 5 | 6 | 7 | 8 | 9 | 10 |

Please help us to improve the course! If we deliver this course again, what should we do differently and why? What do we need to change. Record your thoughts in the Ideas Box below.

Thank you for your help!

Session 10

Top Targets

Stop, Think and Reflect!

What do you need to work on next? Discuss with members of the group and look carefully at your course evaluation. Think of three skills that you'd like to improve then complete the target setting format below.

TARGET 1 The skill I need...	I would use this skill when...	I will know I have improved in this area because...

TARGET 2 The skill I need...	I would use this skill when...	I will know I have improved in this area because...

TARGET 3 The skill I need...	I would use this skill when...	I will know I have improved in this area because...

Signed: ....Date: ....

I will review my targets with .... on........................

This certificate is awarded to:

For successfully completing the Controlling Anger Programme

Well done!
You are a Star!

Signed: ....

Date: ....

Being Me

I fight and I steal, Trimaine's my name,

Causing trouble is my game,

If I spit flame I'll turn you lame,

So I'll always be standing,

I'll never go down,

That is why I'm wearing this crown.

But now I realise,

That it is not wise to tell lies,

And fighting and stealing,

Won't get me anywhere with my dealings,

So now you see,

It is wrong to act like me!

By Trimaine Bailey